Destined for LIFE

THE TRUE STORY OF ONE WOMAN'S JOURNEY

By Lisa A. Bujanda

Cover design by Gil Bujanda
Printed and bound in the United States of America
First Edition

Published by Revive Hope
Temecula, CA. 92592
www.revivehope.net
ISBN-10: 0991156528
ISBN-13: 978-0-9911565-2-8

Dedication

I dedicate this book to my mother Alice Koenke. This book would have never been written if not for your persistence when I was young to seek after God and trust that nothing is impossible for those who believe.

Thank you for instilling in me an unwavering faith to believe God for miracles and for introducing me to Jesus.

Thank you for your constant prayers over the years that have guided me through even the darkest times of my life.

Acknowledgments

Thank you Heavenly Father for all the miracles that you've done in my life. Thank you for carrying me through my darkest hour. There are no words to say how grateful I am for a second chance at life.

Thank you to my husband Gil who walked through this journey with me and who hoped in God against all odds and believed that God would intervene in our lives, even when it seemed impossible. You are amazing and so talented and gifted! Thank you for designing a beautiful cover and helping me to edit this book. I couldn't have done it without you!

Thank You Eric Johnson and Paul Manwaring for the forewords and for your support and encouragement. Thank you to all of those who took time to read this book and write endorsements.

Thank you to my family. I love you!

Thank you to all my family at The Call of Temecula Valley for your support and encouraging me to step out, have a voice and soar. You made this book possible. You are amazing friends!

Endorsements

Trials in life happen, but misery is optional! In this book, the reader will walk with Lisa Bujanda thru some of life's rough winds, but you will gain strength and hope as you see the hand of God working miracles for Lisa. You will be lifted up as you realize that what He did for her, He can do again for you today. I hope you will take some time out of your busy schedule and read this outstanding book —*Destined for Life*. God has a miracle for you!

Roberts Liardon
Author of God's General's
Roberts Liardon Ministries
Sarasota,Florida

I have always said, "People of hope believe that no matter what happens, good is coming!" If you want to be encouraged and filled with hope for every area of your life, *Destined for Life* is for you. Lisa and Gil

Bujanda's story beautifully reveals God's faithfulness no matter how daunting the circumstances may be. I believe they are a prophetic prototype for the type of believer God is raising up today —people who believe in the promises of God beyond what their experience tells them (people consumed with hope that do not know the meaning of impossible). I highly recommend this book.

Steve Backlund
Author of Let's Just Laugh at That
Ignited Hope Ministries
Redding, California

Destined for Life is the true story of the overcoming power of God in the lives of two amazing people. In a world filled with sickness and setbacks, challenges and disappointments, the story of Lisa and Gil Bujanda will empower your faith, restore your hope and enable you to boldly proclaim, "with God, all things are possible." The fingerprints of the Holy Spirit are all over this book!

Michael Brodeur
Author, Revival Culture
Jesus Culture
Redding, Ca

Humanity has been given the precious gift of life by our Father in heaven. God has certainly not promised us a life without challenges, but He has promised to be our ever-present partner at all times. Lisa's story is about one couples journey of learning to partner with God through incredibly difficult challenges. Your faith will be inspired to trust God regardless of the situation or mountain you are facing. It's Lisa and Gil's life testimony, but it can be your prophecy for breakthrough. Prepare to be inspired, challenged, and encounter the goodness of God in your situation. Happy reading!

Abner Suarez
For Such A Time As This, Inc.
Dunn, NC

This endorsement cannot be put in just a few words. Lisa is an amazing woman with an amazing story! I met her about three years ago and immediately felt the love of Jesus from her and her husband Gil!

This book is a must read. Her miraculous story will inspire you. Lisa and Gil's faithful journey to pursue their destiny together, and the testimony of how the Lord has been faithful through difficult lifelong challenges will encourage you to keep moving forward and trusting the Lord no matter how difficult your situation or circumstances are.

Every person no matter where they are in life's journey will come away after reading her story with new courage, faith and strength!!

Wendell McGowan
Kingdom Builder and speaker
www.wendellmcgowan.org
Las Vegas, NV

Find a place to be alone and uninterrupted, cozy yourself into a spot you won't want to leave for a time, and get ready to go on a ride that will open your heart and imagination in ways that you might not have realized were possible! We really need a revelation of Jesus! As you are drawn into Lisa's challenge, disappointment and fulfillment, I believe you're about to have a revelation for yourself —seeing Who He is and wants to be to you! It's a story of dreams becoming promises, transition that yields the fruit of alignment, submission that reveals the gift of God —really, the gift of His love. He loves us so much and invites us into the "Destiny of Life." This is an unsuspecting, riveting journey of His relentless pursuit of our hearts.

Since meeting Lisa and her husband Gil and being in community with them in the early days of the Vineyard, I have enjoyed and been greatly encouraged by their passion for Jesus, hunger for Holy Spirit's presence, love for people, and tenacity for life —pressing through and overcoming, while keeping their eyes fixed on the One on the Throne, who lives in their hearts. We read in the Book of Proverbs that even though "hope deferred makes the heart sick, yet desire fulfilled is a tree of life!" In these pages, you will see how Lisa and Gil not only walk through this and "find Jesus" in the midst of struggle, "against all hope," but like me, you will find yourself lifting the cry from deep within to the One who can and will bring you through, against all odds. He turns the valley of trouble into a door of hope (Hosea 2)!

Lisa, I appreciate the way you faithfully and colorfully unveil the Father coming to you and forming Christ in you. I am stirred by the intimacy and partnership with Him, and that you have said "yes" to the honesty about the real things you've faced that seek to quench God's prophetic dream and invitation. Your own words hit the mark, *"How we choose to walk through the fire will determine the level of victory we will walk in,"* and *"We were a walking testament."* In these pages, I find myself identifying the places of warfare and resistance in my own life while being encouraged to not give up, as well as remembering the dreams and callings God has deposited deep within me, and the longing to really know Him. May you who read this do likewise. I believe you will, hope-filled…

Davis Hill
Firehouse of Prayer
Brea, CA

Contents

Foreword

By Eric Johnson

I met Lisa and Gil a number of years ago at an event here at Bethel. I remember sitting out on the patio after we met and they begin to share the story of their journey. Time would not allow them to share their whole journey in one sitting, but I remember sitting there listening and thinking "Wow, these two are faithful because they know that God is faithful." As we ended our chat I walked away with a sense of gratitude to have met such wonderful people.

What you're about to read is a story of faith. In it you will read about a man and woman's journey of living out faith in all circumstances. Faith is such an interesting thing. As we know, the older we get the more experiences we live through and our faith can become stronger or it can get weaker. The goal of every believer, is for their faith to grow in strength over the years regardless of what takes place. It's one thing to remain full of faith when life is cruising along. There is another realm of faith that can be experienced when life doesn't cruise along nicely.

Recently I have been reading Hebrews 11. In chapter 11, you'll find a listing of different ones throughout the bible that are known for their faith. Some call this chapter the "Hall of Faith". What's interesting to me is when you read the actual stories of who's mentioned in Hebrews 11. There seems to be a difference when you take the story of Moses in the Old Testament and compare it to how it's recorded in Hebrews 11. When you read it in the Old Testament, you see the mother of Moses just trying to save her son and she's makes a basket and puts him in the river. Honestly, that's a pretty crazy thing to do. Think about this, you make a basket and put your infant in it and put it in the river. A lot of things can go very wrong when you put an infant in a basket and put it in the river. She was simply just doing whatever it took, because she was scared for Moses' life. However when God saw that, he saw faith. Moses is recorded in Hebrews 11:23-29, as a man of faith because he forsook Egypt to live among Gods people. In the Old Testament, Moses left Egypt because he murdered an Egyptian and someone found out about it. However God saw this as faith. It's important to remember how God sees things is often times very different than how we see them.

Sometimes in life you are just trying to figure things out as you go and it may not feel like you're doing it out of faith but somehow when you decide to be diligent and wrestle with what's in front of you, it is deemed as faith in Gods eyes. Lisa and Gil lived this so well and they have remained diligent and you'll see they had to figure a lot of things along the way. I have a real strong feeling that Heaven is screaming, "Lisa and Gil are people of Faith, good job faithful ones!!!!"

Eric Johnson
Author, Momentum
and Senior Leader of Bethel Church Redding
Redding, CA

Foreword

By Paul Manwaring

When I picked up this manuscript I thought that I, at least in part, knew the author. But as I read it, I realized, page after page that I had such a limited understanding of her and her husband's incredible journey. Reader after reader will relate to their stories — to the many rich truths and experiences of life that come from just one person and her spouse.

This life story intertwines with many of our journeys; from not believing that miracles are for today, to discovering the truth that they are for today in our beliefs, experience, and practice.

Whoever you are and whatever your life experience has been, this book will give you great hope for your own life as you see through the author's eyes how to access the goodness of God and grow in faith against all the odds.

I saw many parallels of my own life as I read this book, especially in the honor of the skill of doctors. Even though Lisa eventually made the tough decision to walk away from a surgical solution, it was a decision made with wisdom, faith, and under-standing.

I love stories — particularly when I know the person, or develop a connection to them as I read. In this case, both are true. This book carries an invitation for your life story to be rewritten as you read. It does not, of course, invite the kind of trials and challenges that Lisa faced and overcame, but rather to experience the rewriting of any aspect of your life that needs to encounter the goodness of God. This book invites you to shine with the same faith and tenacity that Lisa imparts to us as we read.

Recently my wife shared a verse with me from the Message version of the Bible: *"God rewrote the text of*

my life when I opened the book of my heart to His eyes"
(Psalm 18:24).

This verse is an invitation to each of us and will be amplified repeatedly as you read this incredible story: the story of a woman who was given many seemingly unbearable chapters of her life, and yet every chapter was rewritten as she opened up the book of her heart to His eyes.

Paul Manwaring
Author, What on Earth is Glory?
and Kisses from a Good God
Redding, CA

Introduction

To everything there is a season, a time for every purpose
under heaven: A time to be born and a time to die.
Ecclesiastes 3:1

A week before my 23rd birthday I was near death, and felt my life slipping away. As life drained from my body, an amazing sense of peace came over me and then I heard Father God say, "No, it's not your time". Immediately I felt energy return to my body. Before that moment I was so afraid to die that I didn't want to go to sleep because I feared that I would not wake up. But after this experience I had peace that when my time comes, God will be with me.

As you read through the pages of this book you will join me on my journey through the mountains and valleys of joy and despair. Along the way I discovered that God's hope does not disappoint. The verses from Isaiah have come to pass in my life. God has given me beauty for ashes, the oil of joy for mourning, and the garment of praise for a spirit of heaviness, that I might be called a tree of righteousness, the planting of the Lord, that He may be glorified (based on Isaiah 61:3).

Lisa A. Bujanda

Chapter One

The Bombshell:
The Day My Life Changed Forever

My days are gone, and my plans have been destroyed,
along with the desires of my heart.
Job 17:11 NCV

There are circumstances in life that will change and define us. Like clay on a potter's wheel, our lives are shaped by the experiences and events that make up our lives. But in this process of life there are some moments, especially through tragedy or loss, which catch us completely off guard and leave us begging for answers to the unknown. At one such season in my life, this became my quest —to find an answer to the question *why?*

It was the fall of 1983 —a bright time in America. There was a sense of peace in our country; Ronald Reagan was in the Whitehouse, and I was dating the young man I loved, Gil Bujanda. As an optimistic twenty year-old, I had the rest of my life planned out and to look forward to. Gil and I would get married, have children, and serve the Lord in full-time ministry, going wherever He wanted us to go. It was a great plan! It was our heart's passion —our mission, so we set forth in pursuit of it. But as often happens in life, the best-laid plans get altered along the way.

On October 3rd, 1983 I found myself in my cardiologist's office with Gil at my side. I remember it clearly —it was a day unlike any other. We did our best to try and prepare ourselves for whatever news my doctor was about to give us. We sat there in front of his desk for what seemed like an hour, anxiously waiting for him to come in. In truth, there wasn't really anything that could have prepared us for what he was about to say. His words came crashing into our world like a bombshell as he said, "You have a terminal heart and lung disease". He then began to explain my condition in detailed medical terms, but I couldn't focus on what he was saying. Everything else just faded out. All I could hear were his words echoing through my mind. *Terminal disease. Was this real? Is that what he really said? How could this be?*

In one unexpected moment my life was changed forever. What devastating news! We were just a young couple with hopes of beginning life together, getting married and growing old together. Now suddenly I was being told that I was dying. This no longer felt like the beginning —it felt like the end! My mind was still reeling from my doctor's words when Gil asked the inevitable question; "How much time does she have?" My doctor responded, "Six months …maybe a year". For a moment we just sat there in silence, completely stunned.

In a matter of minutes my future was gone. All those dreams, plans and hopes that Gil and I shared just simply evaporated. *I'm dying.* This was such a grim reality to wrap my mind around. I was devastated. I could barely calm myself long enough to grab my things as we left the office. It was as if we were in a fog —I'm not even sure how we got out of the building, but we found a bench just outside the hospital entrance. The moment we sat down, I burst into tears. I was vaguely aware of other people walking by, but at that point it didn't matter. I was sobbing uncontrollably, and Gil was crying as well. The same questions kept running through my mind: *Why? Why Lord? Why me?* I couldn't believe what I had heard. To make things even worse, as I cried out to God asking Him why this was happening, I felt guilty for even asking why. As a child I had been taught not to question God, but at this moment, facing certain death, I needed to be honest with Him and with myself. It was impossible for me to hide my feelings from Him. I felt abandoned and alone and I needed to hear His voice. *Surely God you have an answer for me!*

From that day forward, more questions began to flood my mind. Even though I passionately served God and pursued His will for my life, I just couldn't believe this was happening to me. *How could God let this happen?* All I wanted to do with my life was to serve God in full-time ministry and raise a family. Now it seemed that none of this would ever happen. There were so many unanswered questions that I was wrestling with. I believed that the answers to these questions were somewhere out there, but I had yet to find where.

When I look back on this time, I can see that I wasn't as alone as I felt. I see a loving heavenly Father who stood by, protecting me throughout my life, guiding me even when I did not sense His closeness. But during this time, I had difficulty reconciling how a good God could let this happen. He seemed so distant now and a barrage of questions kept assaulting my mind. *God, aren't you in control? God where are you? Do you care?*

As the next few days went by, past the unveiling of this dreadful news, I began to think back over my life. I thought about my childhood and recalled the numerous visits to doctor's offices. It was no secret in my family that I was born with a hole in my heart, but

I never imagined that its effects could be so serious. I remembered an incident that happened when I was eight years old as I was competing in a race at school. As my teacher shouted, "go", I ran past all the other kids. Nearing the finish line, I was filled with excitement and anticipation. Then suddenly, I couldn't breathe and I fell to the ground, gasping for air just short of the finish line. As a competitive eight year old, the most upsetting thing for me was that I didn't win the race!

Soon after this incident my parents took me to a heart specialist and I was admitted to the hospital for testing. This stay was extremely traumatic. It was my first time away from home and my parents. The hospital felt cold and sterile, and there was a bad smell in the place. It was one of the best hospitals in the area but to an eight-year-old child, none of that matters. Although I was in the children's ward and there were other kids there with me, it felt cold, dark, and lonely. I remember being terrified on that first night, feeling completely alone.

In those days parents were not allowed to stay overnight because there were so many kids in one room. I remember being so afraid and worried. I kept wondering what was going to happen to me. This first hospital stay ended prematurely, lasting for only three days. A diagnosis could not be given because during the cardiac catheterization I started vomiting. Since the doctors were unable to complete the testing, I was sent home.

I was readmitted to the hospital one month later. This second visit was even more traumatic than the first. There was a little girl in the bed next to mine who was very ill. The divider curtain that separated us did little to lend privacy in the room we shared with the other kids. This poor little girl moaned and cried all night long as nurses hurried back and forth from behind the curtain, trying to make her as comfortable as possible. Not long afterward, during one of the long lonely nights, she passed away and it left me anxious and terrified.

At last the tests were done. My cardiac specialist was finally able to tell my parents what was wrong with me. I had a hole in my heart —a ventricular-septal defect (VSD), which caused a lung disease known as Pulmonary Arterial Hypertension.[1] Together these conditions are specifically identified as Eisenmenger's syndrome.[2] A birth defect caused the hole in my heart (VSD), and this caused oxygen rich and oxygen poor blood to mix. This in turn created extremely high blood pressure in my pulmonary artery and lungs, resulting in irreparable scarring and calcification to my lungs. As Pulmonary Arterial Hypertension progresses, it eventually causes heart failure.

Following my doctor's advice, my parents altered my activities to ensure my safety. I was a happy and energetic child, but I was told that I could no longer participate in many of the things I did for fun, like running races and gymnastics. I had always been very active and I loved to play sports. When I was 6 years old I was in a Spanish dance group —I loved dancing but it was difficult because I was always out of breath. Understandably, this transition was difficult, and I missed doing all the things I loved to do.

As the years went by, I adapted to the changes this interruption to my life required. Even though I was not supposed to do any strenuous activities, I still sometimes ignored my doctor's instructions. In Junior High I loved playing volleyball, but would tire easily and experience shortness of breath. There were other times that I struggled with the limitations of my physical ability, but I still had no clue as to the bleak diagnosis I had not yet been told about. It would not be until years later, in the doctor's office with Gil on that fateful day in October, that I would finally learn the whole truth. There was more to my heart condition than I realized; even worse than the hole in my heart was the fact that I had a lung disease that was considered terminal.

As a child, my parents wanted me to live as normal a life as possible, unburdened by the reality of my diagnosis. I can only imagine what this must have been like for them. I was only told that I had a heart problem and to stop whatever I was doing if I experienced shortness of breath or pain, but I wasn't told how serious it was. Early on, when I was about eight years old, after I collapsed at school, it was determined that sewing up the hole in my heart would not be beneficial because the damage to my lungs was already too extensive. Closing the hole would also put me at greater risk because my heart had already become enlarged to compensate for the lung damage. So my doctors determined that I would probably not live past 15 years of age. Needless to say this was extremely painful news for my parents.

Looking back on the prognosis, I'm grateful that I did not know the seriousness of the situation, because I am certain it would have changed how I lived my life. By keeping this information from me, my parents shielded me from the harsh reality that my life was close to ending. They lived each day aware that I probably wouldn't see my 15th birthday, graduate from high school, get married or have children. But they made the difficult decision not to tell me in the hope that I might live a carefree childhood.

My illness ultimately took a toll on my family; in hindsight I'm able to clearly see how this affected us all. I now know that the hole in my heart was missed at birth —it was a birth defect that should have been detected. If it had been, all that would have been needed was to sew up the hole in my heart. In the 1960's, this was a routine procedure, even for newborns. Furthermore, if it had been caught, my lungs would not have been damaged. The reality of my diagnosis along with its prognosis was a huge burden on my mom and extremely difficult for her to deal with. Not only was her only daughter dying, she was also absolutely helpless to do anything to prevent or remedy it. But at this time, when hope seemed lost, God's light began to shine on my family.

In the midst of impending tragedy, God's goodness intervened. Some compassionate people at my mom's workplace began to share the love of God with her, and talked to her about the hope that is found in Jesus Christ. Through their continued interaction and prayers, my mom became a Christian. It was through these divine appointments orchestrated by Father God, that my mom became the catalyst for my family to encounter God in a new and personal way. This was a life-changing process that powerfully impacted all of our lives. It truly shifted the dynamics and direction of my entire family.

When I was about ten years old, not long after my mom's divine encounter, I remember kneeling down one night to say my prayers. My mom leaned over and asked if I wanted to invite Jesus into my heart, and ask Him to forgive my sins, and give my life over to Him. I remember that night like it was yesterday —my room was filled with God's presence and I could feel a sense of anticipation rise up within me as I replied "yes!" Even though I was just a child, I felt God's presence in a very real way. Over the next days and weeks, I could sense God's love surrounding me even when I was alone. He was with me! I didn't realize it then, but during this time God began to equip me with all that I would need for the long journey that lay ahead. But on that night He filled my heart with hope, igniting a flame that still burns brightly in my heart today.

Now as I look back, I can see that the redeeming hand of God touched my heart that night as He used tragic circumstances to reveal his love to my entire family. Weeks, months and years have passed since that life changing encounter, and it is evident that as I invited God into my life, he took an active role. He watched over me, guided my steps and made my path straight. I managed to get through the rest of my childhood and adolescence without any further crises. Although my physical condition remained unchanged, as I adapted to the necessary restrictions, God's protection kept me stable. If only I knew then what I now know, I would have recognized the hand of God on my life, and His divine protection and favor.

I wonder what my parents must have felt on my 15th birthday. I had outlived the bleak prognosis spoken over my life. I was now a sophomore in high school, fun loving, social, and active. I was involved in so many extracurricular activities that my high school guidance counselor actually told me I wasn't allowed to join any other clubs or activities. I had lots of friends, so high school was a wonderful time in my life —the entire experience was a blast!

I graduated from high school defying the medical odds. Although I didn't realize it at the time, God was building a testimony through my life. Now I know He often chooses the weak things of the world to confound the strong so that His goodness will be seen. But it usually never happens the way we think it should. I wish I knew then, what I know now:

And now I know that God causes all things to work together for good, to those who love God and to those who are called according to His purpose (Romans 8:28 NASB).

He is the Redeemer —but we need to invite Him into our lives and circumstances. He uses everything, including negative situations, and He can turn circumstances around, even the impossible ones!

As a teenager and young adult, I was serious about pursuing a relationship with Jesus Christ and growing in the Lord. When I was twenty years old I began dating my soon to be husband, Gil. But after we started dating my health began to deteriorate.

July 4th, 1983, was a hot and smoggy Southern California day. Gil and I had gone out to a local lake with some friends for a picnic. As we sat there in the scorching sun, I began to have symptoms that I had never experienced before: my lungs felt tight and I could barely breathe. I had chest pain and became too exhausted to move. I attempted to brush it off, as any resilient twenty year old might do, but the symptoms became so pronounced that I had to be carried back to the car. In the air-conditioned car I rested and gradually recovered, but this incident unnerved me and left me with many unspoken questions. *What's happening to me? What caused me to lose all energy and not be able to breathe? Is there something more serious going on with my health?*

Throughout the summer of 1983, the symptoms continued to worsen despite my attempts to ignore them. After weeks of battling fatigue, chest pain and shortness of breath, my body wore down. At this point, I was working as a junior buyer for a local company in Pasadena, California. One day while at work I suddenly felt faint and couldn't catch my breath. As I laid my head down on the desk, my energy level plummeted, and I almost passed out. No matter how much I tried to calm myself and breathe, I simply could not get enough air. I felt like I was suffocating! I could no longer dismiss the symptoms that were overwhelming me. Now, for the first time, I knew without a doubt that something was really wrong.

So now, somehow, I needed to get to the hospital but I didn't want to create a scene. My supervisor offered to drive me to the hospital, since it was only a few miles away. While I should have accepted her offer, I didn't want anyone to know that I might be seriously ill. So I gathered some strength, left the office, and drove myself to the hospital emergency room. In hindsight it's amazing to see the sense of resolve that rises up in a person when fear and adrenaline kick in. But no amount of resolve could stop the tears from streaming down my face. My hopes for the future were being eclipsed by fear of the unknown. It all felt hauntingly familiar, sitting there once again in the sterile halls of the hospital where I was diagnosed just

12 years earlier, remembering the traumatic times I endured there as a little girl.

When I arrived at the emergency room I was turning blue. I was immediately put in a wheelchair and then hooked up to oxygen. After monitoring my vitals, the ER doctor excused himself to contact my pediatric cardiologist who was still on staff at the hospital. When he returned, he looked troubled. I don't remember much of what he said except that it was extremely important for me to see my cardiologist as soon as possible. He also said "your disease is getting worse". I didn't understand what he meant, but I was not alert enough to ask more questions. Although rest and oxygen eventually provided some relief, I felt that I knew even less than when I walked into the hospital earlier that afternoon. The questions that began hounding me weeks earlier now returned in full-force. But even more distressing than these unanswered questions, was the fear of the unknown.

This brings us back to the beginning of this chapter. It was in that moment, sitting in my cardiologist's office with Gil that we both encountered the brutal reality of shattered hope. As I mentioned earlier, we left that office devastated, feeling like the rug had been pulled out from underneath us. We were told I was dying! How does someone deal with that kind of news, especially at 20 years old? Everything that my doctor said seemed like he was referring to someone else —it was hard to believe he was talking about me. He said the symptoms I was experiencing were signs of deterioration, which indicated that the lung disease I was initially diagnosed with was getting worse. Now, as a young adult, I was finally given full knowledge of my condition along with its predicted outcome. It was terminal and there was no known cure.

Back then, in 1983, there was a new transplant surgery that was being developed at Stanford University in Palo Alto, California. They were experimenting with heart-lung transplantation (the heart and both lungs in the same surgery). [3] In an effort to provide me with some hope, my doctor urged us to look into the program. It was a new development that was still in the experimental stages and offered no guarantees. So we began the process and submitted my name for consideration.

By this time, Gil and I were planning to get married. But we now faced staggering problems and needed to make life-altering decisions without clear answers available. Time seemed to be running out as the negative medical reports kept coming! We were told a number of times that without the heart-lung transplant, there was no hope for my survival.

Even though we were committed Christians, we felt that somehow God had left us. We felt alone, out of control, afraid and confused. But just as Abraham did, hoping against all hope, we continued to hope (Romans 4:18). We held on to the little bit of hope that still remained in our hearts. None of what we were experiencing made any sense. We were so young — we were about to start our lives together and we were filled with so many dreams. We couldn't just give up, especially now that there was so much to live for.

It was at this time, as we took hold of those few fragments that were left of our shattered hope, that we anchored ourselves in God. Gil and I pushed past our despair and began to pray together. We now realize that this began the momentum that would eventually lead to a turn around. In our new and now highly complex life together, we were being forged by circumstances beyond our control. Prayer became our source of sustenance and strength, and we discovered that it was to be my lifeline in the long journey ahead. We chose to pray and hope together. If we were to find answers, we were determined to find them in God. Despite all of our uncertainties and desperation, we chose to believe and hold on to hope.

Endnotes

[1] http://en.wikipedia.org/wiki/Pulmonary_hypertension

[2] http://en.wikipedia.org/wiki/Eisenmenger%27s_syndrome

[3] http://en.wikipedia.org/wiki/Heart–lung_transplant

Chapter Two

Happy Ever After?

"For I know the plans I have for you," declares the Lord,
plans to prosper you and not to harm you,
plans to give you hope and a future".
Jeremiah 29:11

When I was young, my mother and I would pray for my future husband. Of course I didn't know who he was at the time, but that didn't stop me from praying for him. As I got older I prayed that God would give my future husband a vision —a picture of me as his wife, and that this man, whom I would spend my life with, would reveal this vision to me as a supernatural sign. I didn't want to make a mistake and I didn't trust my own judgment. I really wanted it to be God's choice because I knew it would be the best choice. I think it's amazing how God can take a simple heartfelt desire and bring it into reality. I believe He even sometimes places these prayers in our hearts just so He can answer them!

I didn't know it then, but God was already at work answering my prayers. In 1980, a year before we met, Gil encountered God in a very powerful way and became a Christian. By the summer of 1981 Gil was going through an extremely difficult time. Over a two-week period, he was constantly asking God if he would ever be happy. One day as Gil was working on a ladder while hanging light fixtures, God answered. He had a vision, a simple picture of me in a wedding dress. He also heard "This is your wife." It was very clear, so clear that Gil even wondered why it was in present tense. Because he was still a young believer, he didn't know what to call this experience (a vision, with a word of knowledge). But he knew this was the answer to his prayer for happiness. And for the first time after months of struggling, he felt peace and a strong sense of God's presence. Visions and words of knowledge were not a common occurrence in Gil's life at this time. He was still a young believer and unfamiliar with the different ways that God speaks. But the vision startled him so much that it almost knocked him off the ladder. I like to say that's when he first fell for me!

A few days later Gil and I saw each other at a party for mutual friends. It was toward the end of summer and I was preparing for my second year of college. By now, I was feeling a strong sense of direction in my life and doing well in school. A group of young people from our church had put together this party for some of our friends that were moving away for the new school year. My personality was like a butterfly; at gatherings like this I would float from one person to the next, engaging in conversation. I enjoyed meeting new people and was outgoing and fun-loving. The night was a typical southern California summer evening, and Gil was outside sitting on a chase lounge. Although we were just acquaintances at the time, I approached him and I asked what God had been doing in his life. It was just an icebreaker kind of question but he replied that the

Lord had shown him who he was going to marry. He went on to say "but I don't think she knows yet". I was shocked by his response but also intrigued, so I encouraged him. I told him it was great news and that if it was really God, He would also reveal it to the girl as well. I shared an encouraging story regarding a young man and the vision he had about his future wife —it was very similar in fact. I had absolutely no idea that my encouragement to Gil had anything to do with me; it never even crossed my mind! As previously mentioned, I was heading back to another year of college, and marriage was not on my radar.

During that second year of college, I would return home on weekends and go to church. There were two guys on campus that were interested in becoming more than friends, but I made a decision not to date anyone at this time because of a previous relationship. I wanted to make sure that I didn't make another mistake, so dating was not at the forefront of my mind. I knew that when the time was right, I would be ready. I occasionally brought these two friends from school to church, but Gil was undaunted. Later he told me he could see that they liked me, but he had peace and would think; *they don't have a chance!*

Eventually Gil asked me out. The movie *Chariots of Fire* had just come out and after church one day all of our friends were talking about it. It was one of the first movies with a Christian theme to get international attention. Since I was extremely busy with school, I hadn't seen it yet. I was taking 18 units at the time and I was also the university's yearbook editor. There were also community outreach projects that every student was required to participate in. So I was really busy and didn't have a lot of time to go out. I expressed my interest to see the movie, and Gil graciously and selflessly offered to take me to see it —before anyone else had the chance to offer. I still had no idea that his vision was about me, or that he had other motives for taking me to the movie. So Gil drove out to my school and we saw *Chariots of Fire*. It was fantastic and we had a good time together. As we drove back from the movie, Gil asked the Lord if it was time to ask me out for a real date. The response he got back was a clear "not yet". So he dropped me off, said goodbye and for the next few months we only occasionally saw each other at church.

I don't know how Gil was able to keep quiet about his vision for so long. To this day he doesn't like to keep surprises secret; he gets so excited that he ends up telling me about them in advance. So I believe it must have been God helping him to be patient and wait for the right timing. If Gil had told me earlier that I was the girl in the vision, I probably would have freaked out and said "no way". I was not ready to get married and it would have scared me off.

On Memorial Day weekend of 1982, nine months after our conversation at the party, our church scheduled a weekend retreat up in the mountains. As I prepared to go to the retreat, I was asking God about my future. I knew He was preparing someone for me and I had been waiting on His timing as I asked for direction. So as I went up to the mountains that weekend, I asked God if either of the two guys from school might be my future husband. But I was in for a big surprise by the end of that weekend!

It had been a few months since Gil and I saw the movie, and the weekend retreat began on a Friday night. The mountains of California can be stunningly beautiful, but that weekend it was kind of cold. Gil knew that I was going to be there, so he was also praying and asking "Lord, if it's your time for us to get together just let it happen —encourage me so that I know it's you".

As Gil got up early on that Saturday morning, he discovered that he had a huge welt on his nose. He didn't know it at the time, but this was an allergic reaction and his entire nose was swollen, red, and tender. To make things even worse, he had recently resorted to wearing his old "coke bottle" glasses because he didn't have enough money to buy a new pair of contact lenses. As Gil woke up and looked into the mirror that morning he thought; *God, this is really going to have to be you now!* The funny thing is I think that God must have blinded me to it, because the entire weekend I never noticed the thick glasses or his swollen nose!

I got up to the retreat center early on Friday and Gil arrived later that night. I was staying in a room with four other girls. I'm usually the last one up in the morning because I'm not a morning person, but I didn't want to be late for the first session that morning, so I was the first one up and in the shower. Once I was ready for the day, I went over to the main lodge. And wouldn't you know it, the only other person there was Gil, so I sat down next to him and we started talking. Morning devotions were before breakfast, so it was natural for us to go in together since none of our friends had come in yet. It ended up that Gil and I spent the entire retreat hanging out together.

At the end of the weekend Gil asked if I would talk with him before we left. So we walked up to a romantic little spot nestled in between some beautiful cedar trees and sat down on a bench. The wind was blowing through the trees and the air was cool and crisp. As we started to talk, Gil asked if I remembered last September, and the vision he had when God revealed to him who his wife would be. Nervously I said "yes" (gulp). He said, "Well, um, it's you". I was speechless, actually more like dumbfounded. Then the Lord reminded me of my prayer, "Give my husband a vision of me and then have him tell me". I believe to this day that God put that prayer in my heart because He was laying out His plans for us. Isn't God amazing? I had gone up the mountain asking God about my future husband. I was asking if it might be one of the two guys from school. But God had chosen Gil and in that moment I knew God answered my prayer and Gil was to be my husband. Of course, I didn't tell Gil at the time. I needed to be sure, so I waited a few months. Then Gil asked if when we got down the mountain, if he could call me and we could go out on a date. This always makes me laugh, because I thought, *well, since we're getting married I guess we need to get to know each other first.* Nothing like putting the cart before the horse! It was completely backward by every standard but looking back we realize why God did this. He answered our prayers, and arranged our marriage. He had a future for us!

We started dating after the retreat, and fell in love. Although we had different personalities and dispositions, we were matched in our love and devotion to God. I was still going to school, so I would regularly come home on weekends and spend time with Gil. About eleven months after we started dating, on a Sunday afternoon in April of 1983, we prayed something that changed the course of our lives forever. We said "God, we give you permission to do whatever it takes to make us most useful to you". I have to say that prayers like this should come with a warning label. Whatever you do, don't pray this prayer unless you really mean it —God takes it seriously! Gil and I were in his parent's living room and prayed that prayer, giving our hearts and lives totally to God. We no longer just wanted to fit God into our lives; we wanted our lives to fit into His plan. That day we dedicated our lives to Him for His service and His purposes. With youthful passion and uninhibited surrender, we asked Him to do whatever it takes to make us the most useful in His Kingdom. It was a divine appointment. God marked us that day and in that moment we felt the Lord calling us into ministry. Naturally, we thought our next step would be to go to seminary, or start some type of formal training. But little did we know our training at the University of Consuming Fire had just begun. Just as Joseph was first sold into slavery before he saw his dreams come into reality, God's preparation often precedes times of God-ordained fruitfulness. It was the prison that prepared Joseph for the palace. We heard the call of the Lord and responded. We joined the ranks of God's army, and now boot camp would be our next stop along the way. We didn't realize it until years later, but what we prayed on that April afternoon at Gil's parent's home was a pivot point. God answered our prayer and took us up on our offer. The preparation for His service had begun! Our lives would never be the same.

Chapter Three

Bride Banks on Waiting List

He gives strength to the weary and increases the power of the weak. But those who hope in the LORD will renew their strength. They will soar on wings like eagles; they will run and not grow weary, they will walk and not faint.

Isaiah 40:29-31

Despite the devastating news we received on that dreadful day in October of 1983, we made the decision to be married. We believed that God put us together so we decided to continue with our plans. Even though my cardiologist gave me just six months to live, Gil and I went shopping for a ring. Back then Gil didn't make enough money to support us, so we were praying for a better job for him. In the meantime Gil and I moved forward in faith and set out in search of the perfect wedding ring and we got engaged on November 12, 1983. Amazingly enough, the very day Gil picked up the ring from the jewelry store, a major utility company called him for an interview! This was completely unexpected because Gil had put in the job application a year earlier and had completely forgotten about it —but God didn't forget! God answered our prayers and was guiding our path. Gil went for the interview and got the job on November 21, 1983, one week before my 21st birthday. With this new job, he immediately doubled his income —what a birthday present!

It was a year of many firsts for us. Gil arranged a surprise birthday party for me. I never had one before and all my friends were there. This was a good time for us —we were about to be married and I was so excited. Even though I was still experiencing fatigue and shortness of breath, for a few brief moments, I could forget about the dire circumstances of my life. During the next few months I was so preoccupied with wedding plans that I didn't have time to dwell on the death sentence still hanging over my head.

My body however, was constantly trying to pull me back into reality. I began to feel more and more ill, until I could no longer work. At first, I reduced my hours to part-time, but after a few months I couldn't even handle that. So my doctor made the decision to put me on full disability. He said that I was deteriorating rapidly, and that once this process started it was irreversible. His words hit me hard, bringing me face to face with the undeniable fact that I was dying and there was nothing I could do to change it. I was physically and emotionally exhausted. I slept for days only waking up to eat, use the bathroom, and answer Gil's phone calls.

Even though we were in the middle of excruciatingly difficult circumstances, we were determined to press through. We set a date to be married; September 8, 1984. It seemed that every time we were faced with an obstacle and made the choice to keep moving forward, God gave us the grace to walk through it all. Although my body was weakening, I started to feel joy as I had something to look forward to. We found a cute little place to rent that was close to many of my friends from church. It was a quiet piece of property with six small cottages built in the 1920s. We lovingly dubbed it Christian Corner because a few other young married couples from church also lived there. I moved into our little place in June of that year and my maid of honor temporarily moved in with me. I was eagerly anticipating the biggest day of my life, but as the time drew closer, I became more and more anxious; *would I physically be able to handle the wedding ceremony and reception? Would I be able to enjoy our honeymoon?* So I prayed and asked the Lord for direction. To my astonishment He gave me an idea that answered my concerns. Just ten days before the wedding I thought; w*hy not have a small ceremony in our new home, before the big wedding?* So one week before we were to be married in a large church ceremony, we had a small wedding at our little house at Christian Corner. Everyone in both of our families supported this decision. Our pastor, the wedding party, and our immediate family members all gathered together in our home and shared this special occasion with us. It was a simple, intimate wedding on a beautiful day —a perfect answer from God that dissolved stress and anxiety. Everything went as planned, except during the ceremony I attempted to put Gil's ring on the wrong hand. I was embarrassed, but everyone else got a good laugh out of it. So after we got married, we went off to the rehearsal dinner. Again, in our usual style, we put the cart before the horse! We had fun that week with the sequence of events that led up to our big church wedding. The morning of the big day we got up, giggling at each other, saying, "Well, let's go get married". Other than those involved in our small ceremony the week before, none of our guests knew that we were already married. I guess now the secret is finally out!

September 8, 1984 turned out to be one of the hottest days of the year in sunny Southern California. But I felt the love and prayers of our friends and family that had gathered together to celebrate this special day with us. The presence of the Lord was evident, along with His joy and peace. God's idea had worked! We were both able to enjoy our wedding with our families and 250 of our closest friends. It would have never crossed my mind to have a small wedding before the big wedding day. It was only after I asked God for a solution that I received an answer. Papa God is filled with fantastic ideas that He freely shares if we just ask for His help!

When we returned home from our honeymoon, reality was there to greet us as we stepped inside the front door. Despite all the love and joy I was surrounded by, my symptoms got even worse. We certainly were not your typical newlyweds. We had to face the cruel fact that I still had a death sentence looming over my life. At the time we were so young that we didn't really know how to deal with such a serious situation. I was only 21 years old and Gil was barely 24. We tried to stay as close to the Lord as we could —it was the only sure thing we knew to do.

A few weeks into our marriage, Gil and I began to talk about the specifics of the heart-lung transplant surgery. In 1984, Stanford University in Palo Alto, California was the only place in the world that was experimenting with the heart and double lung transplant. My doctor wanted to have me evaluated as a potential transplant patient because I wouldn't be accepted for the surgery unless some preliminary testing was done. So the evaluation paperwork was submitted and we waited to see if I would be chosen for testing. People from all over the world were waiting for the surgery, and we ended up waiting for a year and a half before we heard from Stanford.

In the meantime, we were also advised that if I was going to have the transplant surgery, fundraising efforts would be necessary. Transplantation of the heart and lungs was still in its infancy, and was not covered by insurance companies. For the transplant and other costs it would be hundreds of thousands of dollars. Included would be additional costs for extended hospitalization and medication. Gil and I would also have to relocate to Palo Alto, because I would have to be close to the hospital (for the rest of my life). This was such a huge undertaking and one that we could not manage on our own. We didn't have that kind of money but my life was hanging in the balance —we knew something had to be done. My doctor along with the medical community agreed that the transplant was my only hope. If successful, it would buy me time, but no one could say how much.

We were also told that the success rate for the few surgeries that had already been done was good and that the new generation of anti-rejection drugs was promising. What we didn't realize at the time was that many of the reports published in the medical journals were somewhat premature. There was a need for increased funding to continue research, so the early reports painted an overly optimistic picture. We were never thrilled about the surgery, but at this point we thought it was my only hope for survival. Our church pulled together and began a fund-raising campaign to cover the cost of the surgery. Local television stations, newspapers, and neighboring churches were contacted. My story began to spread throughout the San Gabriel Valley and then eventually aired on Los Angeles TV news along with Newspaper articles.

Heart transplantation was a hot topic in the news at the time. There were many new and innovative heart transplant procedures that caught the attention of the world. One such surgery was the xenotransplant procedure performed at Loma Linda University Medical Center in Southern California. It involved an infant known as Baby Fae, who had hypoplastic left heart syndrome (HLHS). Baby Fae became the first human to receive the heart of a baboon and this was making headlines all over the world. Sadly, Baby Fae died only 21 days after the surgery due to rejection of the transplanted heart. [4]

For a few months Gil and I were kept busy with interview after interview and God gave me strength to go through each one. As we saw ourselves on TV programs, TV news, and read our story in the L.A. Times, reality sunk in even further. It was unnerving to watch myself on the evening news as a reporter asked my doctor, "How much time does she have left?" My doctor responded, "She has no time left and without the transplant she will die." A headline in the L.A. Times read "Bride's Life Depends on Waiting List, Heart-Lung Transplant Only Hope for Alhambra

Woman". How was I supposed to process this? *God, is this for real?*

Immediately after we completed the fundraising media push, Gil and I hit rock bottom. We sunk into intense desperation and despair. During this time, my life seemed to be at a standstill. It was difficult for me to watch the lives of my family and friends moving forward. They were so full of life. Many of our young newlywed friends were now having children. Some were finishing college or buying their first homes. But despair and tormenting questions began to plague me. *Would I ever have a chance to live again? Would I be able to move past this, or was this really the end for me?* Everyone around me seemed to be living life and having fun. I was supposed to be right there with them, but instead my life had come to a screeching halt.

Needless to say this period of my life may qualify as the most challenging ever! The changes in my life were polar opposites; I experienced the most wonderful highs, like getting married, and also encountered the most devastating lows and the most challenging moments of my young life up to that point. I was being stretched as I learned to navigate through extreme circumstances in such a short window of time. I felt like I must have experienced the entire gamut of human emotion during this time. But I continued do everything I could to fight for my life and to hold on to God in the process.

Endnotes

4 http://en.wikipedia.org/wiki/Baby_Fae

This article appeared in the Los Angeles Times on December 9, 1984

Chapter Four

Losing our Theology and Finding Jesus

Then you will call upon me and come and pray to me,
and I will listen to you. You will seek me and find me
when you seek me with all your heart.
Jeremiah 29:12-13

As I repeatedly told my story to the media over the course of two months, I became even more desperate for answers. We were still newlyweds and we should have been enjoying the honeymoon phase of marriage. Instead, our first few months of married life were characterized by emotional turmoil, more questions, and desperate cries to God for help. *Would Gil and I have a future together? Or would Gil have to face the future alone so soon after marrying me?* Every night I would pour my heart out to God, through tears of pain and hopelessness. I cried so much during this time that it seemed like my eyes were rarely dry. Although I know differently now, I felt like God was sitting up in heaven judging the world and had no time for me. I felt so broken and alone that I lost hope. I thought I had a personal relationship with God, but now He felt so far away. Everything Gil and I believed was being challenged. Could I believe that God was good and yet still be going through this terrible, life destroying process? But it was our desperation and need for answers that drove us toward God. It would have been easier to become offended at God and blame Him for everything. I understand why people do that, especially when they experience circumstances that seem unfair. But if we permit it, God will use even unjust and unfair circumstances to reveal more of Himself to us. So Gil and I began to pray together every night. I asked questions that only God could answer —"Do you care about me? Will I have a future? Can I trust you?"

I sometimes felt like giving up and just dying. At least then, my struggle would be over. But on the other hand, I wanted to live and have a family just like my friends. Their lives seemed to go on; but mine was hanging in the balance. It felt so unfair. I would go to church on Sunday and come home crying because people began to ignore me. They just didn't know how to deal with my situation. They didn't know how to relate to someone who was dying, especially someone so young. This made me feel even more alone.

During this time many of our well-intentioned friends, family, and church were praying that the Lord would guide the surgeon's hands (during the transplant surgery) or also praying that God would help me accept the process of dying. This began to trouble us, and at a certain point we wondered why no one was asking God to heal me through supernatural intervention, like we read of in the Bible. So Gil and I asked God for ourselves: "God, do you still heal today?" As a child I was taught to go to God for everything and ask for His will in every situation. We realized that we hadn't done this —we went to other sources first, namely the medical field. I have heard Paul Manwaring, a pastor at Bethel Church in Redding California say "surgery is not a second class healing." I completely agree with this, so I'm not saying that God will not use doctors to heal people. But Gil and I simply realized that we did not consider divine healing as an option. So it became clear that we should at least present the question to God. If we truly believed in a God who could do anything, then we should at least give Him the opportunity to do what only He can do. It just made sense.

When I was a child I believed in the supernatural power of God, but as I grew older, an unbelieving mindset crept in. By the time I was a young adult I had unintentionally acquiesced to the subconscious belief that while God *can* do anything, He probably won't. Both Gil and I were taught that miracles are like a bolt from the blue, and we should not seek after them. By agreeing with this mindset, our minds became fertile ground for believing lies about God. Lies that say God had somehow changed and was no longer the same. But God says of Himself: " *For I the Lord, I do not change* (Malachi 3:6 NKJV), and the New

Testament book of Hebrews says, *"Jesus Christ is the same: yesterday, today and forever"* (Hebrews 13:8). This is extremely good news when you need a miracle! Our knowledge, understanding and personal revelation of God can (and should continue to) change, but He Himself does not change.

At church we would sing the lyrics of a worship song: *"You are my hiding place, you always fill my heart with songs of deliverance. Whenever I am afraid, I will trust in you"*. But what I was being taught in church didn't seem to line up with those words. Could I trust and truly believe that God would deliver? I wasn't ready to die and God wasn't giving me the peace to accept death. So as Gil and I pursued God, as we continued to read our Bibles and pray, God met us. He began speaking to us about His heart and His kingdom. He was renewing our minds by changing the way we thought —changing our theology. We were awed and amazed! The Bible began to come alive and we realized that it was loaded with the supernatural healings and miracles which were recorded to serve as a reminder of what is still available today.

We continued to cry out to God. By now we were so desperate to know Him and hear His voice that we were ready to throw out everything we thought we knew; our theology, our doctrinal bias, and our man-made ideas. We began having times of focused prayer every night, asking God to speak to us. We didn't want to risk missing out on anything He had for us, due to ignorance, bad theology, unbelief, doubt or any other hindrance. Our position was one of surrender. We would pray "Do whatever it takes, teach us, speak to us. Tell us what *you* have to say about our situation". We prayed along these lines for months. And through persistent prayer, laying our hearts before God, the Lord began to reveal His heart to us. Both Gil and I had a deep personal revelation of God's love. We fully opened our hearts and minds to Him in this place of encounter as He revealed Himself to us. We found that when God's love becomes a personal reality, it's easy to believe Him for anything! Imagine that —the most powerful being in the universe loves us!

John 10:27 says, *"My sheep listen to my voice, I know them, and they follow me"*. This was one of many verses that guided us in this time. The Holy Spirit continued to highlight even more verses like the following: *"Ask and it will be given to you, seek and you will find, knock and the door will be opened to you. For anyone who asks receives, and he who seeks finds, and to him who knocks the door will be opened"* (Matthew 7:7-8).

Matthew 7:9-11 was also a powerful promise to us as well: *"What man is there if his son asks for bread, will he give him a stone? Or a fish, will he give him a serpent? If you then, being evil, know how to give good gifts to your children, how much more will your Father in heaven give good things to those who ask Him"*. Any good human father would not want to see his child sick and suffering. He would take them to a doctor and help them get well. In the same way, our Heavenly Father wants us to be well. *It is the enemy of our souls who comes to steal, kill and destroy; but Jesus comes to bring life and life more abundantly* (John 10:10 paraphrased).

How can anyone believe that God wants to make His children sick? If any earthly father made their child sick we would have them arrested for child abuse. If it's God's will for us to be sick; then why would we even go to a doctor to get well? That would be going against God's will. If in our experience we find that not everyone gets healed of their sickness and suffering it doesn't mean God doesn't want His children to be well. 2 Peter 3:9 NKJV says *"The Lord is ...not willing that any should perish but that all should come to repentance"*. So we know that it is God's will for every human being to come into right relationship with him. Yet we don't see this facet of God's will realized in every person's life. Regarding salvation for our souls, most Evangelical Christians do not have a problem with the concept that people must trust and believe God in order to receive salvation. I believe this very same principle can be found throughout the Bible, including when it comes to healing for our bodies.

In Psalm 103:1-5 (NKJV) we read, *"Bless the Lord, O my soul; And all that is within me, bless His holy name! Bless the Lord, O my soul, And forget not all His benefits:*

Who forgives all your iniquities, Who heals all your diseases, Who redeems your life from destruction, Who crowns you with loving kindness and tender mercies, Who satisfies your mouth with good things, So that your youth is renewed like the eagles."

In reflecting on this verse, the Holy Spirit showed me that in His Kingdom, there is actually a benefits package! He forgives all our sins and He heals all our diseases, He redeems our life and satisfies us with good things. And in Matthew 15:21-28, we find the story of the Canaanite woman who asks Jesus to heal her daughter. Part of Jesus' response includes a peculiar reference to physical healing as being the "children's bread". We are those children, and healing for our bodies is part of the diet of Kingdom-centered believers.

Before the Holy Spirit highlighted these verses to us, we had been taught that miracles in the Bible were necessary in the early church because they didn't have a New Testament like we do. This line of reasoning advocates that the early church needed miracles in order to believe in Jesus and successfully evangelize. But again, the Holy Spirit reminded us *"Jesus Christ is the same yesterday, today and forever"(Hebrews 13: 8 NKJV).*

All that we read of in the New Testament —the miracles Jesus performed, the power of God available to the early church —this is also available to us now. It was not Him who changed, but us. Cultural mindsets and popular misconceptions have negatively impacted the church from its beginning. Many Christians, even to this day just stopped believing in the supernatural power of God to save and to heal. In the New Testament, the Greek word *sozo* (σῴζω), Strong: G4982, is primarily translated as *to save*, but it also has other meanings. It can also be translated as *to deliver, to rescue, to heal, to cure, or to restore to health.* The salvation Jesus obtained for us brings healing to every part of us, body, soul & spirit. This is Biblical salvation —the power of God to save our souls, to physically heal us and to deliver us.

As God continued to speak to Gil and I individually about healing, at first we were hesitant to tell each other what God was revealing. On April 7th, 1985 we finally compared notes, and realized we had both come to the same conclusion: God was asking us to believe and trust Him for healing. We discovered that we had a Father who cared for us personally. We started believing God's Word over our own intellect and experience. As we stood on the truth that God is the same yesterday, today and forever, we were baptized in a new found joy and the depression that hung over both of us dissipated. We felt like we had received resurrection power from God!

"But if the Spirit of Him who raised Jesus from the dead dwells in you, He who raised Christ from the dead will also give life to your mortal bodies through His Spirit who dwells in you." (Romans 8:11 NKJV)

We laughed and said we felt like we had become born-again again. We had gone through the dark night of the soul and now the dawn was breaking. This just happened to be on Easter Sunday of 1985.

Both Gil and I experienced a deeper understanding of what resurrection life is about, and the reality that it is still available today.

We now fully embraced the truth that God had provided physical, emotional and spiritual healing for us, through the cross of Jesus Christ. This is a complete salvation for body, soul and spirit. We began to believe in the Jesus of the Bible —the one who heals and the one who saves. As a result, my image of Father God began to change. I no longer saw God as sitting far off in heaven judging everyone, or as an unpredictable deity who was usually in a bad mood. I was now able to see Him as a loving, merciful and compassionate Father who wants to heal His children. Our reasoning and theology were thrown out the window and God replaced it with the good news of the Gospel of the Kingdom.

In the Lord's Prayer it says *"Our Father in Heaven, hallowed be your name, your Kingdom come, your will be done on earth as it is in heaven"*. (Matthew 6:9 NKJV)

As a child when I would recite this prayer, I somehow misunderstood it, thinking God had two separate wills: One for earth and another for heaven. But we realized Jesus is simply saying, when you pray, ask for God's Kingdom (His government, rule, reign and authority) to be released onto the earth, and for God's will that is being done in heaven to come to earth. God has the same will for heaven as He does for earth. We pray for God's will to be done on earth just like in Heaven. Is there sickness in Heaven? No, then He doesn't want sickness on earth. It's God's will to heal His children. His will does not change because He never changes! The church therefore is the primary way that God releases His will to the earth —first through prayer and then through acts of service. This powerful truth revealed to us through the Lord's Prayer is a key to the Kingdom. We realized that prayer is one of the primary means that God has given believers to release His will to the inhabitants of earth. Unfortunately, it is one of the most underused keys in the church.

It was now the Monday morning after Easter. I was sitting at the kitchen table in our little cottage at Christian Corner. As I started to pray out loud, the next thing I knew, I was praying in a language I had never heard before. Just as in the Book of Acts on the day of Pentecost, I received the gift of tongues. When I was a child I asked God to give me this gift, but at the same time I was somewhat afraid of it. Later as I got older and my theology changed, I decided I didn't really need this gift after all. It seemed too weird and besides, it didn't make sense to me. But that morning, God gave it to me anyway. As I was praying in the Spirit, in this new prayer language, I could now hear Him even clearer than before.

That day, God reminded me of a dream He had given me a year earlier: One night in May of 1984, four months before I got married, I was praying and crying out to God for hope. I just wanted to be happy and to have the pressures lifted from my life. I asked Him for hope, and to hear His voice through the flood of circumstances of my life. I asked God to speak to me through dreams or any other means. That night I had a dream that was the answer to my prayers. In the dream I was at my grandmother's house and my mother was sitting in the dining room crying. When I asked her why, she said because of a Bible verse God had given her for me. She said "you can't pour new wine into old wineskins or the skins will burst and the wine will spill out and the wineskins will be ruined. You can only pour new wine into new wineskins". In this dream, my mother took the verse to mean that the transplant was not going to work and I would die. Immediately I felt the Lord say that she had misinterpreted the verse. He said to me "I will give you a new heart and new lungs. And when I pour out the new wine into your new wineskins they will not burst but both will be preserved." I consoled my mother in the dream and told her that God was going to heal me. Immediately when I woke up from the dream I went to find the verse. I wasn't familiar with it and didn't know where it was in the Bible. The verse was Mark 2:22, and as I read it, the words came to life and I got excited. It was my first indication that God wanted to supernaturally heal me. I was so excited that I told someone on the leadership team at my church, but she responded, "You can't rely on dreams." Then she went on to say that I was taking the verse out of context. The encouragement and promise that God tried to give me through that dream was quenched. My heart was downcast as I quietly tucked the dream away —that is until this morning on April 8th, 1985. That day God also reminded me of a promise he had given me when I was only 12 years old which says, "*I will give you a new heart and put a new spirit within you; I will remove from you your heart of stone and give you a heart of flesh*" (Ezekiel 36:26 NKJV).

My response to these promises was important. I needed to be like Moses and not waver in the promise. Romans chapter 10 says, "*So then faith comes by hearing, and hearing by the word of God*" (Romans 10:17 NKJV). I needed to stand in faith and believe. A key verse at this time was "*All scripture is God-breathed and is useful for teaching, rebuking, correcting and training in righteousness, so that the man of God may be thoroughly equipped for every good work*"(2 Timothy 3: 16-17 NIV).

God's grace and mercy was fully directed toward me at this time, as He gave me one verse after another to stand on. He also gave me what I now consider to be my life verse: *"I shall not die, but live and declare the works of the Lord."* (Psalm 118:17 NKJV).

It is difficult for me to fully express through words the powerful awareness of God's presence that I had during this time. His Word came alive to both Gil and I. We heard His voice clearer than ever before and we experienced His presence in our lives in a fresh, new way. I think I can imagine how the disciples must have felt on the day of Pentecost when they received the Holy Spirit with tongues of fire on them. These experiences gave me greater insight into the magnificent glory of what a relationship with God can be like.

Chapter Five

Against All Hope

I would have lost heart, unless I had believed
That I would see the goodness of the Lord
in the land of the living.
Psalms 27:13 NKJV

God's amazing love gave us a greater sense of expectation. Hope had all but evaporated in our hearts, but was now being restored. Romans 4:18 speaks about the Jewish patriarch Abraham and the circumstances he faced: "*Against all hope, Abraham in hope believed and so became the father of many nations*".

Our days and nights of grief and hopelessness were ending. We couldn't keep this kind of news quiet —we wanted to shout it from the rooftops! My weeping had been turned into joy and both Gil and I began to share with others what God was doing in our lives. The Lord had just done a remarkable thing and we began to tell anyone who would listen. But the response we got in return was unexpected. Our joy was met with opposition, and our faith was met with fear. I couldn't understand why everyone wasn't happy for us —I was no longer going to die! But some of our closest friends and family began correcting us, fearing that we were embracing false hope. Some went so far as to say that what we believed was not scriptural, even heretical. Others just stood back in doubt, fear and unbelief. We were hurt and confused. Heresy was such a strong word. Were we deceived? *Does God really speak to ordinary people in this day and age?* Or were we simply in denial and ignoring an inevitable outcome? But the more we continued to seek God and read the Bible, the more we came face to face with the reality of the supernatural. But the big question was: is that supernatural reality still available to believers today? We were determined to find out, and to hold on to what we believed God was saying to us. So despite the continued opposition, we strengthened ourselves in the Lord. The more we stood in faith and put our trust in God, the more convinced we became that God wanted to heal me. This was such a season of transition for us —there were still emotional highs and lows, but our faith in God's willingness to heal continued to increase as He further revealed His heart to us.

God's empowering presence was on us, preparing us for what was up ahead. Quite amazingly, during this time He put people in our lives that came alongside and encouraged us. Gil began working with a young man who was also a strong Christian. As Gil shared our story, this young man was so moved that he asked if he could come over and pray for me. He became a great encouragement to Gil, continually sharing verses from the Bible and expounding on them. A short time later, another of Gil's coworkers asked to come over to pray. He came with his wife and some friends from their church. As we sat down in our living room to pray, they asked if they could lay hands on me, and then they prayed for God to heal me. This was the first time we experienced anything like this. We now have words and terms to describe what happened, but back then all we knew is that there was a tangible increase of faith and hope. It was an amazing experience. They called it "soaking prayer" and I always felt stronger after they left. Although these new friends lived over an hour away, they visited a few more times, always praying with us. We were deeply encouraged by the love and support they brought.

Meanwhile, despite our growing faith, and increasing resolve to trust God for healing, we were being dragged down by the environment around us. We continued to have run-ins with people from our church. Some of them could not perceive what God was doing in my life, and felt that it was their duty to correct us. This made us all the more thankful for those friends and family members who were able to offer faith and hope during this time. But by now, we knew for certain that our pastor had heard reports of our alleged heresy. So in an attempt to explain what was happening to us, we scheduled an appointment. We hoped he would be able to support what God was doing in our lives, and what we were being shown in regard to healing. We prayed for a positive outcome for this meeting, but we had already been met with so much opposition from others in our church that our expectations were low. The meeting was fairly short, and ended abruptly when we were told: "you cannot believe that and still come to (this) church". There wasn't much we could say to that. Presented with such a strong ultimatum our choices became clear. We left that meeting disappointed but not surprised, and for the sake of my life, we made the painful decision to leave our church. We decided to stand in faith, and trust God's leading, even if no one else stood with us. We left that church misunderstood, judged as believing heresy, and even shunned by some. And all this because we believed in the truth of God's Word —that He restores and He heals. This was an extremely difficult fork in the road for us. This was the church Gil's family members were saved in, and my family was there as well. We both served in the church from its early stages and helped to see it grow. Both of our families and many of our friends were either in leadership or in some type of ministry there. We also lived at Christian Corner, which further complicated an already difficult situation. This was our first home as a married couple —a little community of other young couples from our church family. It had been a place of love, peace and comfort but now it became a place of loneliness, isolation and rejection. For a period of time we were ignored, rebuked, or avoided because people didn't understand or know how to respond. In a way, it was like experiencing another level of death —the death of cherished relationships with people we had grown to love and depend on. I was still dealing with serious physical symptoms, and all of this just added more layers of difficulty, complicating an already unbearable situation. We now knew there was only one direction to go —toward God. And so we pressed on.

Shortly after we left our church, the Holy Spirit began to open our spiritual eyes to an even greater degree. We saw things in the Bible that we had read before, but now it was as if we were seeing them for the first time. Verses began to jump out at us, or were highlighted in special ways. We heard God so clearly now, and this helped soothe the sting of rejection. But God was still working to bring about reconciliation, at least to some degree. One day, while visiting a couple from our now former church, the conversation took a turn, and we were admonished for embracing bad doctrine. As the conversation was about to explode into a full-blown argument, I just had to speak up; I could sense the presence of God so strongly. I reminded them of the man in the Bible who was healed of blindness. When he was bombarded and harassed by unbelieving questioners, he replied "all I know is I was blind and now I see". I then said "All I know is I was depressed and crying all the time. Now I have hope & joy. I was dying with no hope and now I have hope for the future. The Lord has spoken to us and we have decided to stand on His Word". The room got very quiet. And then everyone began to cry. The Holy Spirit cut through all of the arguing over theology and went straight to the heart of the matter —the reality that God cares about us. Even though we may not have had words for it back then, I think everyone recognized God in that moment. I will never forget His presence and power in the room that day.

It was a transitional moment that I will remember forever.

We needed to be around people who believed in healing, so we decided to attend Church on the Way, in Van Nuys, California. We were familiar with Jack Hayford, because a few months earlier we started listening to his messages on the local Foursquare radio station. We noticed that we were always strengthened and uplifted by his messages, so attending Jack's church seemed to be a natural choice. We loved that church and the power of the worship. Every time we attended we came away with a deeper understanding of how good our Heavenly Father is. It took over an hour to get there on Sunday mornings, so ultimately the drive was too much for me. I was still very weak, and it was difficult for me to be away from home for more than a few hours at a time. We knew we needed to find a church closer to home —a church that prayed for and believed in healing. At the urging of one of Gil's friends from work, we visited a local Vineyard Church. The minute we walked into the building we both sensed the Lord saying "*this is home"*. That first day we introduced ourselves to our new pastor and shared some of our story. We were amazed that he sat with us for nearly an hour after church, encouraging us to stand and believe.

It was now June of 1985. Over the next few months, the Lord began to address areas of our souls that needed healing. We had both been through so much —even traumatized by the rollercoaster ride of events of the last year and a half. Within the safety of our new church family, we learned how to forgive others and in that process we received healing from the wounds of rejection and pain. As we continued attending our new church, our individual relationships with Father God deepened. For the first time both Gil and I were being taught in practical ways, how to hear God. We began to develop the spiritual side of our Christianity. Jesus said in John 4:24 (NKJV) *"God is Spirit, and those who worship Him must worship in spirit and truth"*. We already believed that truth was found in the Word of God, in Jesus and the Bible. Now we were finally beginning to understand this deep eternal truth; Father God wants to have a deep spiritual connection with every human being. This truth is at the heart of the Christian message.

One Sunday at Church, the Lord spoke to me during worship. People all around were singing, *"Nothing I desire compares with you"*. As I sang out, in a posture of worship and surrender, the Lord showed me that I desired physical healing more than Him. He was drawing me closer to Himself, and so He exposed one of the things that had eclipsed my desire for Him. He said, "Seek me first and all these things will be added to you, including your healing." So as I embraced God's gentle correction, I asked the Lord to help me to learn how to always seek His face and not just His hand.

At our new church, we were learning and growing. We were building new relationships and walking through life with a group of people that embraced the things God was showing us. Every Sunday, people would pray for me, lay hands on me, and speak prophetically over my life. During the week, prayer teams would also come to our house and pray for me. We now had a family of believers who stood with us for my healing, and together we sought the face of God. Gil and I continued to learn many things about the presence of God and the Holy Spirit. We were growing spiritually and learning to walk in the deeper things of God. We were incredibly blessed and experiencing transformation. God was taking all of the difficulties we had gone through and turning them around for good.

One day while at church, I was praying for a lady who wanted to be healed. As I laid my hands on her, I sensed the presence of God in a new way. I felt heat and power flowing through my hands, and much to my surprise, she was healed! I had never before felt such a sensation, nor had God ever used me to heal others. That encounter was such an encouragement for both of us. Even though I was not yet fully healed, God still used me to bring healing into another person's life. God used that situation to get my attention and remind me that nothing is impossible for Him.

I was reminded of these verses found in 1 Corinthians 12: 4-11 (NASB): *"Now there are varieties of gifts, but the same Spirit; and there are varieties of service, but the same Lord; and there are varieties of activities, but it is the same God who empowers them all in everyone. To each is given the manifestation of the Spirit for the common good. For to one is given through the Spirit the utterance of wisdom, and to another the utterance of knowledge according to the same Spirit, to another faith by the same Spirit, to another gifts of healing by the one Spirit, to another the working of miracles, to another prophecy, to another the ability to distinguish between spirits, to another various kinds of tongues, to another the interpretation of tongues. All these are empowered by one and the same Spirit, who apportions to each one individually as he wills"*.

God uses people as a conduit of blessing. That is what the gifts of the Spirit are for. He uses anyone who is willing. What an amazing gift and privilege!

Chapter Six

"It's Not Your Time"

But the eyes of the Lord are on those who fear him, on those whose hope is in his unfailing love, to deliver them from death and keep them alive in famine.

Psalm 33:18,19

Testing reveals the true strength of any foundation and late in the summer of 1985, Gil and I entered the most severe season of testing we had ever experienced. We now realize that when God gives someone a clear promise, the realm of darkness tries to come in and nullify that promise. This information would have been extremely useful for us to know at the time, but we were learning as we went along. The testing of God's promises over my life was about to begin, and I was unprepared for what was about to happen. Was I willing to trust in God no matter what?

Would I be able to hold on to the hope that he had given me? We had been married for a year and just as the doctors predicted, my physical condition worsened. At the lowest point I was so weak that I was not able to get out of bed without assistance. I was on oxygen 24 hours a day, battling chest pain, arrhythmia, and literally gasping for air to breathe. I felt drained of energy to the point that I could hardly move. As I lay there day after day, it was unbearable, because although my body was weak and failing, my mind was still alert. One of the few things I could still do was think, and I now had endless hours each day to think about everything. As I wrestled with what I was feeling, I felt so trapped. I felt betrayed by my body —even imprisoned by it. At times I couldn't speak because it took too much energy. This was such a contrast from where I was just a few months earlier.

As a teenager, I was active, outgoing, and involved in all sorts of activities and events. I was very social and liked being around people. This now made it even more difficult to be trapped at home. I was used to being independent, but now I couldn't take care of myself without assistance. I was dependent upon others for just about everything —I had trouble even raising a glass of water to my mouth. It was agonizing! Although people were there to help me, I still felt utterly alone. On many nights I would cry myself to sleep. It got to the point that I was afraid to be left alone because I didn't want to die alone. I felt like that was all that was left to happen now, and it was terrifying. Something had to change, but how? I literally depended on God for every breath, but once again, there were times I couldn't sense His presence or hear His voice.

The physical and emotional pain was more than I could handle. Each day, I felt like I couldn't take the suffering one more day. But even at this low point there was a flicker of hope that would not go out —the seed of promise that God planted in my heart. He continued to give me strength to hold on for one more day and then one more day after that. He gave me what I needed day by day. When things got really bleak, Gil and I would sometimes resort to humor. I wish I had written down more of the gems we came up with. One of my favorites was "When you're at the end of your rope, God gives you more rope". As bad as that sounds now, it was my reality and seemed really funny at the time.

At times fear would overwhelm me: fear of suffocating (because that's what it was like with no oxygen getting to my lungs), fear of living in pain or a prolonged period of suffering, fear of never getting out of bed, fear of going to sleep and not waking up, and fear of taking my last breath. During the times when fear became more real than hope, I would try to center myself and focus on God's Word. This became a very tangible source of strength for me. One of my favorite verses, which I would remind myself of constantly says, *"Fear not, for I am with you; be not dismayed, for I am your God. I will strengthen you, Yes, I will help you, I will uphold you with my righteous right hand"* (Isaiah 41:10 NKJV). I held on to this verse, even though my mind was still racing with questions.

I would spend the hours thinking and talking to God. I was no longer afraid to ask questions, even the tough ones. I discovered that He can handle it. I would ask, "Where is my healing? And what about your promise to be with me through everything?" Looking back I can see that at my weakest point, God gave me strength to go on, and to persevere. *"He gives strength to the weary and increases the power of the weak. Even youths grow tired and weary, and young men stumble and fall; but those who hope in the Lord will renew their strength. They will soar on wings like eagles; they will run and not grow weary, they will walk and not be faint"* (Isaiah, 40:29-31). The truth is, He was always with me. It was just difficult for me to see that during this time.

I was now confined to home now, so the only time I saw people was when they came to visit or to pray for me. This brought great encouragement, and helped to break up the seemingly endless hours that made up each day. Another thing I did to pass the time was to put on some headphones and fill my mind and spirit with worship songs and listen to the Bible. I didn't realize it at the time, but this was one of the most powerfully practical things I could have done. Not only did this strengthen my mind and spirit, but it also helped me to keep my focus on God. With my focus on Him and the truth of His promises, it became difficult to dwell on circumstances, or the fear I was battling. I positioned myself right where I needed to be, resting in the goodness of God. I learned that what we give our attention to influences the spiritual atmosphere around us. If I wanted to live in and experience hope, I needed to feed myself hope. It was a simple concept, but without making this decision, I don't believe I would have made it through this time. I fought to keep my faith and hope in God fully intact.

Every night Gil would lay his hands on me and pray. We would pray for healing and for strength to continue the unrelenting battle. As the battle raged, we often felt like we were losing. But I now see that God was there, with me through it all. His promise to never leave me or forsake me was true. We may not have always understood, or felt like His promises were real, but truth is not dependent upon feelings. At some point all of us face situations where we simply have to make a decision and say, "God, I choose to trust you no matter what I am feeling. I choose to trust you no matter what I see. I choose to believe that you are good, and that you love me".

I would also draw upon the faith that my mother instilled in me when I was a little girl. I remembered her saying, "God is the only one you can entirely depend upon and trust. Lean on Him." I learned how true that statement was during this time. He was the only one I could fully depend on. My life and strength could only come from Him. He is the giver of life, He is the foundation of strength, and He is always there in every moment especially when we don't sense Him. During the hours I spent alone, I would also sing the words to a favorite hymn I learned while growing up: *"Turn your eyes upon Jesus, look full in his wonderful face and the things of earth will grow strangely dim in the light of his glory and grace."* These love-filled words of worship brought peace to my soul. I did not realize it then, but I was learning to encourage myself in the Lord.

As my health deteriorated, Gil planned to take me to the hospital, because there was a new procedure that my cardiologist wanted to try. If successful, it was hoped that it would help me to breathe better. It was a last ditch effort because my blood had become so thick from a lack of oxygen that something needed to be done, and soon. So the plan was to drain my blood and replace it with blood that had been thinned with plasma. But as the hematologist attempted to drain my blood, even after multiple attempts he just couldn't do it. My doctor then came in and tried as well. There wasn't any logical reason as to why this would have happened; it was a simple enough procedure and catheter placement was common at this time. I believe now that God just had other plans for me. If this procedure had been successful, I would have needed to repeat the process every few weeks for the rest of my life. What a horrifying prospect! After the catheterization attempt failed, my doctor asked Gil whether I would be more comfortable in the hospital, or at home. Because I already had oxygen and the medication I needed at home, Gil said I would be more comfortable in my own room. In truth, there wasn't anything more they could do for me at the hospital that couldn't be done at home. I was still months away from being called up to Stanford for the transplant candidate evaluation, but my body was now failing. So my doctors sent me home. Although they never said so, I know they sent me home to die.

My cardiologist continued to keep in touch with Gil. Two weeks later, at Gil's request, he actually came to our house. This was very unusual because house calls were already a thing of the past. My doctor examined me and then took Gil into another room and spoke with him. He began to console Gil, asking him to not view death as a loss, but to see it as a graduation. With empathy, he also advised Gil to get everything in order, and to make arrangements because he said I would most likely die within the next few days. As the doctor left our house, Gil went into the living room and began to sob. He slumped down on the floor and as he cried out to God he remembered the vision of me in a wedding dress. Gil began to pray and said "God, you gave her to me, and I don't

believe you gave her to me just so I could take care of her the last year of her life. You said I'd be happy". Then suddenly, the Lord directed him to Psalm 40. As Gil read it, the verses came alive: *"I waited patiently for the Lord; he turned to me and heard my cry. He lifted me out of the slimy pit, out of the mud and mire; he set my feet on a rock and gave me a firm place to stand. He put a new song in my mouth, a hymn of praise to our God. Many will see and fear the Lord and put their trust in him."*
(Psalm 40:1-3)

Gil knew that God had given Him a promise —we would get through this! Even though we were in a slimy pit, God would turn it around. God gave Gil strength and endurance to hold on to, despite the doctor's bad news. On the human level Gil experienced all of the emotions that would be expected, but on a spirit level, something changed. There was now faith where only fear and hopelessness were before. That afternoon, Gil was given an infusion of God-birthed hope.

Gil did not tell me what the doctor said that day or about his interaction with God. A few days after the doctor came to our house, right before my 23rd birthday, I felt like the struggle for my life was coming to an end. One night with Gil by my side, I told him that I loved him and that I felt like I was going to die soon. That night I was wide-awake because I couldn't sleep. My chest was hurting despite the pain medication and nitroglycerine for the angina. I also slept with a pillow propped up because I was still gasping for air, even while using oxygen. Later that night, as Gil finally fell asleep, I felt energy leave my body and my life slip away with it. The peace I felt at this moment was indescribable. I felt like I was suspended between two realms, almost buoyant or floating. And then I heard God say, "No, it's not your time". Instantly I felt energy return to my body and in just a matter of seconds I was solidly back in my body. This, I believe was the transitional moment that I had been waiting for. It would take a while before it became evident, but something had finally changed.

"For He has not despised my cries of deep despair. He is my First Responder to my sufferings. And didn't look the other way when I was in pain. He was there all the time, listening to the song of the afflicted". (Psalm 22:24 TPT)

Looking back, these few months were the worst time of my life; even writing about it stirs up so much emotion. But it also reminds me of how thankful I am to God for His grace and His faithfulness, especially during this time. He truly rescued me from death and set my feet on a rock, in just an instant, a brief transitional moment. My heart sings of the truth of 2 Corinthians 12:9, *"For my grace is sufficient for you, my strength is made perfect in weakness".*

Chapter Seven

Death Sentence Suspended

I shall not die, but live and declare the works of the Lord.
Psalm 118:17 NKJV

It was now the beginning of a New Year, January of 1986. A month had passed since I experienced God's intervention that night in my room. I gradually went from being unable to get out of bed, to being able to get up and walk around for short periods of time. It was quite a change in just a few weeks. We scheduled a doctor's appointment, but were very apprehensive about this check-up. We felt like we couldn't take any more bad news so we just wanted to keep our minds focused on what God was doing. We believed that something was happening, and we didn't want to be talked out of it. After the doctor examined me, he went out to the waiting room to talk to Gil. By this time, he was an older man, ready to retire. Gil said he was almost running as he stepped into the waiting room. Excitedly, he asked, "what have you been doing?" Gil was caught off guard, and replied, "What do you mean?" My cardiologist went on to explain that there was improvement in 5 different areas and then said, "This isn't supposed to happen —this disease is irreversible!" Gil then said, "We've been praying", to which the doctor asked, "What have you been praying?" Gil felt like he was being asked to recite a magic prayer that my doctor could use on other patients. But instead Gil said, "We're just asking God to heal Lisa". The doctor seemed stunned and then said, "Well whatever you're doing, keep doing it because it's definitely working". On the drive home, we kept thanking God, alternately laughing and crying, filled with gratitude for all that God was doing. In the months that followed, I continued to gain more strength as we walked in the promise that God had given us.

Some time had passed since that day in the doctor's office and it was now the spring of 1986. I finally received the call from Stanford University. They were ready to see me, and wanted to start the process of evaluation for the heart-lung transplant program. By now we believed God was going to complete the healing that had begun and I would not need the transplant. But we wanted to make an informed decision. We had never spoken directly with the surgeons or people that were actually performing the transplants. We really didn't know what the surgery entailed, or how it would affect the rest of my life. So we flew up to San Jose, rented a car for the day and drove to the hospital in Palo Alto. We were ready for whatever the day would bring.

The day was long and grueling, filled with one test after another, including blood and tissue typing as well as interviews with team members. All of this was necessary to determine if I would be a good candidate for placement on the heart-lung transplant list. When we arrived at Stanford earlier that day, we did not know what to expect or what the outcome would be. We just knew that we needed closure to this part of our lives. By the end of the day, after all tests and evaluations were completed, we finally met with some of the surgeons as well as the department head of surgery. They explained to us that there had only been ten surgeries done with people who had my diagnosis, and that Stanford was the only hospital in the world doing them at the time. They were at the forefront of heart-lung transplantation, and it was still considered to be in the experimental stages.

At the end of the day, Gil and I met with the head surgeon, just the three of us in his office. He spoke openly with us, beginning with statistics. He said that five of those ten individuals died, either during the surgery or shortly thereafter. There were also four others who were very ill and their bodies were rejecting the newly transplanted organs. These were put back on the transplant list to have the surgery done over. There was only one woman who was still living but her quality of life was poor because of the massive amount of drugs she was on just to reduce the ongoing threat of organ rejection. We were also told that if successful, the life expectancy after the transplant was five years or less. The head surgeon went on to explain that the medical reports, and articles in medical journals painted an overly positive picture, which in turn made way for further funding. This was the only way to continue to experiment and perfect the surgery. He was also very candid regarding what we would face both during and after the surgery. I would need to be on a massive amount of drugs to suppress my immune system, because the chance of organ rejection would always be present. In effect, it would be like not having an immune system. I would always need to wear a mask and stay away from children, pets and sick people. In addition, I would have to stay away from crowds; so going to the movies, malls or church would be off limits. Gil and I were also asked if we were willing to move to Palo Alto, so we could be close to the hospital. There would be constant testing and check-ups for the rest of my life. This was not the life restoring operation we were told of —it would completely alter any hope for a normal life.

This was already so much information to process, but then the head surgeon finished by saying, "You're a good candidate because you are well enough to handle the surgery. The procedure is still in the experimental stage, but you would also be helping future patients with the same condition to have a better chance of survival." *Wow, did he just ask me to be a human guinea pig?* The final thing he said to us on that day was remarkable. It was another one of those moments that we will never forget. He said, "If you have any other hope go with that". I thought; *did he really just say that?* Medically speaking there wasn't any other hope. It was considered a terminal disease. The heart-lung transplant was the best hope humans had to offer. At this point we turned to him and said, "Yes, we do have another hope. God is my hope." We were asked to go home and think about it since we didn't need to make a final decision that day. So as we got up to leave, we thanked the head surgeon. We are so grateful for his honesty and integrity.

We got back on the plane that evening feeling an amazing sense of relief. Instead of feeling devastated or disappointed, Gil and I felt overwhelming peace and we were actually happy. God had been guiding us all along. This day could have been such a huge setback, but it became a doorway and we stepped through it. *No turning back now.* We were at peace now and comforted by God's guidance in our decisions over the last two and a half years. We were glad that we hadn't sunk all of our hope into the transplant as the primary means to save my life. This much was now clear; God was now the only one who held my future in his hands. Ultimately, this is the one truth that can bring lasting peace people's lives, but not everyone recognizes this. Gil and I were just blessed enough to have our circumstances bring this into focus.

Today there are better anti-rejection drugs available and heart transplantation itself is very successful. But lung transplantation is still risky and still has a prognosis of five years or less.[5] At this point, I want to reiterate, I am not opposed to doctors or surgery. I believe God uses doctors to heal people. And if in my case, surgery could have given me a healthy long life, I probably would have done it. I just believe it's important to ask God what He wants to do, and in my case, this was the question that saved my life.

God's love and faithfulness continued to be revealed in my life. As the days and months went by, I progressively got stronger and healthier. I was not completely well but I was getting stronger day by day and I believed God would complete the healing. By the time summer came, I was riding my bike three miles a day. I was feeling so much better and felt physically rejuvenated. In a period of just eight months I went from being bedridden and dying to exercising and living a fairly normal life. It was such a dramatic difference. Gil and I were amazed and I daily thanked God for every breath.

During this time, Psalm 91 spoke clearly to me: *"He shall call upon me, and I will answer him; I will be with him in trouble; I will deliver him and honor him. With long life I will satisfy him, and show him my salvation"*(Psalm 91:15-16 NKJV).

This verse became real to me —I called upon the Lord and I now had His answer. Even though these two and a half years proved to be the most difficult time of our lives, they serve as a constant reminder of God's goodness and faithfulness. I will forever remain thankful and in awe to God for His grace and His faithfulness during this time of my life.

Looking back over this long journey, I can now see how God carried me through each step along the way. At every turn, He was there strengthening and guiding me. I remember the story of Corrie Ten Boom, along with her sister Betsy. While in a German concentration camp during World War II, Corrie confided in her sister that she feared death. Betsy responded, "Remember what our dad said to us; do not worry, God will give you the ticket when you need to board the train". There is such truth in this statement. God gives us exactly what we need just when we need it. 2 Peter 1:3 reminds us of this kingdom principle: *"His divine power has given us everything we need for a godly life through our knowledge of Him who called us by his own glory and goodness."*

I learned so many things through this process. First and foremost, God's ways are not our ways. Gil and I had to change our expectations of what it meant to receive from God. We learned how to take what God was showing us through our relationship with Him, and by that we were strengthened in faith and guided. God began to change the way we thought, because His answers don't usually come the way we expect. We need to keep ourselves open and not put Him in a little religious box. Everything is possible for Him, but the way we think, believe and perceive has an effect on what we are able to receive. In my case we thought that God would either heal me instantly or I would go home to heaven. Instead, the healing came progressively. But in the process of letting go of our assumptions, we learned some extremely valuable life lessons. And more importantly, we became personally acquainted with God and were able to experience Him.

To this day, God continues to be my healer and my quality of life increases every day. He is the One who sustains me. According to medical standards, I'm not completely healed, but my quality of life has drastically improved. I did not succumb to death but was restored to life. I don't have an answer as to why healing has been such a slow process, but I have learned to be at peace. God causes all things to work together for our good. And each situation, each challenge and each conflict is an opportunity for Him to display His goodness. He can squeeze the good out of even tragic, horrible situations *if we let Him*. It's as if He waits for us to invite Him into our circumstances. I believe He waits, eagerly anticipating that time when we give Him permission, when we invite Him in, and He says "ok, now let me show you what I can do with this".

"All things work together for good for those who are called according to His purpose" (Romans 8:28 NKJV). No matter what comes at us, Papa God can turn it around for good. Bill Johnson, a Pastor at Bethel Church in Redding, California says it best, *"God can win with a pair of twos."* Today, I do not believe that God causes disease or sickness. Nor do I believe that it is His will for us to suffer through disease or sickness. But we

live in a fallen, broken world. And until we invite God into our situation, we can suffer and be subjected to the effects of the fall. I think that if most people examined what they really believed in regard to this, they'd land in the same place I have. If you believe it is God who makes you sick, or that it is God's will for you to be sick, then please, do not violate His will by trying to get well or by taking medicine, or by going to a doctor. But most of us go to a doctor anyway, even if we believe God made us sick. Ultimately, it's difficult to pray with faith for healing, if you believe God doesn't want you well.

So through these years, Gil and I learned what it meant to persevere and overcome in the face of monumental obstacles. This process of healing and walking it out in faith helped to develop things in our character that are priceless. God did work all things together for our good —even using those things that He was not the author of.

Endnotes

[5]http://www.ustransplant.org/annual_reports/current/113_surv-new_dh.htm

Chapter Eight

The Earth Cracks Beneath Us

Fear not, for I am with you, be not dismayed, for I am your
God, I will strengthen you, yes I will help you, I will
uphold you with My righteous right hand.
Isaiah 41:10 NKJV

Although God causes all things to work together for our good, this in no way guarantees that life will be easy! For Gil and I this was evidently clear. It had barely been a year since the supernatural encounters with God that radically changed our lives. But during this year we felt like we were constantly bumping our heads against an invisible ceiling, as we continued to experience opposition from people in our former church. At this point we wanted to begin a new chapter in our lives. We wanted the freedom to think for ourselves, and right or wrong, we needed to be able to make our own decisions even if it resulted in mistakes. And so, we found ourselves once again at a transition point.

We wanted to buy our own home, and felt like it was time to move out of the area that we had both grown up in. As we began praying and seeking God for direction, we came across a flyer for a new master planned community about 90 miles away from where we lived. The advertisement got our attention, so one Saturday morning we decided to investigate.

As we entered the Temecula Valley, we were caught surprised by its beauty. The sky was vibrant blue and the air was clean. Back then, in February of 1987, the area was mostly rural and mountains surrounded the valley. There were a few wineries and dairy farms, and just a few traffic lights in the entire town. It was so inviting, but even more than this, from our first visit we sensed God drawing us there. We had both lived in the city all our lives, but the beauty of this valley was breathtaking and we instantly felt connected to it. We found a little house and began the process of buying it. A few weeks later on the drive back home —after signing for the loan, we sensed the Lord saying "not this one". We knew that if we heeded the "no", no matter how disappointing it was, it would clear the way for something better. By now, we had learned to trust His voice, and so we called the sales office and cancelled the sale.

A few months later we resumed the search for a new home. At one point, we thought we would just buy a little piece of land and place a mobile home on it until we were ready to build. The cost of new homes had risen in the short time since our first visit. It became so discouraging, that we stopped looking. But we had to trust that God's timing was better than our own. At that point, a man in our church gave us a prophetic word. He said, "God says get ready to move soon." We kind of laughed it off, and didn't give it much thought. With our budget, it didn't look like we would be moving anytime soon. As we began to look again, it proved to be a true word. Just a few weeks later, we found a newly built home that we could afford, and within a month we moved to Temecula.

From the beginning of this process, God worked out a number of things that enabled us to buy our first home. He gave me strategies that I would never have thought of. He gave us favor all along the way. We were so excited to move into our very first home and start a new life in an historic area with a growing community. The area was slow-paced and peaceful. There were some gorgeous mountains that we could see as we looked out of our bedroom. There was a historic old town that went back to the Pony Express era, and the area was also becoming a weekend destination for wine lovers. There was also new development going on with what was called a "master planned community". The week we moved in, I remember walking into a grocery store, and the cashier welcoming me to town and saying, "you must be new here". It was a warm and inviting community and we were happy to become part of it.

After just two short weeks, as we were beginning to settle into our new home, we came face to face with an earthshaking challenge as we literally experienced the earth cracking beneath us. As it turned out, our new home was built on an active fault line! One of our new neighbors just a few houses away noticed that the pavement on our street had cracked and we discovered that this crack went through our property. In our back yard, the crack was about two inches wide, but so deep that we could put a broom handle down inside it —and could have dropped it! Once again we found ourselves on TV news and in the newspapers. We were one of a handful of families to move into the new neighborhood, so immediately after the news broke, all escrows were stopped. Out of the 40 or so homes that were built, only six had been moved into. Our neighborhood was almost completely empty for the next two years, as the builder, geologists, and lawyers tried to find out what had happened and if anything could be done to correct it. This became a major challenge for us —our dream house was now a worthless property that we could not sell or move out of.

Interestingly enough, as we were buying the house, I asked if there were any earthquake fault lines near our property. Maybe it seemed like an odd question, but living in California it's a good question to ask. The realtor replied "no", but soon after it became apparent she was misinformed. Once again we began to seek God's intervention and direction. One of our new neighbors contacted an attorney, and began a class action lawsuit. At first we were hesitant to get involved, but as the weeks went on, the various companies involved began blaming each other and we felt like we were being ignored. So we decided to join our neighbors in the lawsuit.

It had only been a few weeks since we found out our home was built on an active fault line. We were trying desperately to gain some sense of normalcy in our everyday lives, so we carried on the best we could. But on October 1st, 1987, a major earthquake shook most of Southern California. The Whittier Narrows quake caused eight fatalities, injured several hundred more people, and left property damage estimated at over 358 million dollars. This main quake was followed by almost 500 aftershocks.

On the day of the main earthquake, Gil and I had driven out to my family's house for the day. Later we learned that my parent's home was located just one mile from the epicenter of the quake. I grew up in Southern California and was familiar with earthquakes, but what we experienced on that day was so powerful that it felt and sounded like a bomb had gone off. I had never been in a quake of this magnitude before —it was horrible and frightening.

The largest aftershock on October 4th caused even more damage to weakened buildings. Connecting fault lines in the Temecula Valley were also affected, and we felt the earth violently shake that morning while we were at home. All of the seismic activity, coupled with the fact that our new home was built on an active fault line, precipitated the onset of what I now know were anxiety attacks. As the earth continued to rumble, I no longer felt safe at home. With every aftershock, the anxiety attacks grew worse and worse, to the point that I would have them continuously throughout the day.

Although I had improvement from the heart and lung symptoms I experienced two years earlier, these symptoms were different. Anxiety attacks make you feel as though you are going to die: you perspire, your heart races, and it feels like your heart is going to pound itself right out of your chest. And so now, once again, I found it difficult to breathe. As the anxiety disorder progressed, I became agoraphobic. I didn't want to leave my house because I was overwhelmed with the fear that I would have an attack and not be close enough to a phone to call for help. Back then mobile phones were still not common. Looking back, I now see that I fell right into the trap that the enemy had set for me. I allowed fear to grip me and neither Gil nor I knew what to do about it.

We were still under enormous stress because of the situation with the house. The litigation process was extremely stressful and we thought we would lose our new home and all the money we had put into it. We didn't know if we would lose everything now, including a place to live. I had sold my car so we could have enough money to buy the house, so now I was alone at home during the day while Gil was at work. I was in a new area, and really didn't know anyone. And Gil was still working almost 70 miles away, because a transfer had not come through yet. So I began driving out with Gil as he left early in the morning to go to work. I would stay at my family's house until he got off work just so I wouldn't be alone.

Before the earthquakes, I had never heard of anxiety attacks, and had no idea what they were. I endured the attacks for over six months before I finally discovered what was happening to me. One day, in total discouragement and hopelessness, I told Gil to just commit me to a mental hospital. But instead, we made a decision to take a weekend away from our circumstances and attend a marriage conference up at Pismo Beach, which some old friends had invited us to. I was hoping to get my mind off all the problems that consumed me, and just wanted an escape from what I was experiencing. So I thought getting away would be a good diversion, but I had no idea how difficult that weekend would end up being. We still didn't know that I was experiencing anxiety attacks

—we somehow thought that these new symptoms were related to my heart and lung disease.

Gil and I had high hopes for our weekend together, away from all the stress back home. But as we drove up the coast, I began having severe attacks —the worst I had experienced up to that point. I couldn't breathe and had gone into full-blown panic! There were long stretches of empty road and coastline as we headed toward our destination. It seemed like there was nothing for miles at a time. Anxiety consumed me and I kept wondering; *where is a hospital? What if I pass out?* Once again, death seemed like a very real possibility.

Once we arrived, I wasn't able to leave the hotel room and go to the conference room. We were at a nice hotel overlooking the beach. It was peaceful setting, but I didn't feel any peace. I had just made it through some extremely difficult years, walking through impossible challenges, but with God's help I overcame. Now, I found myself in the middle of another major challenge. It was all so overwhelming;

was I doing something wrong? Was there a huge target on my back? And what could I do to make it all stop?

God promises to never leave us or forsake us, and on that weekend, despite all the challenges, we realized just how true this promise is. God is always working on our behalf, and this season of my life provided more evidence of that truth. Our trip up the coast was a set up! It was a divine appointment, and once again, God was causing all things to work together for our good. One of the men attending the conference was a Christian psychiatrist who specialized in anxiety and panic disorders. He had even published a number of articles. He also happened to be a friend of the friends that invited us to the conference. Once he heard about what was happening, he came up to the hotel room and asked me to tell him about what I was experiencing. He then explained that I was having anxiety attacks and it was more than likely related to my heart condition. He said that when I have palpitations, it causes my heart to send a panic message to my brain. This caused me to go into full-blown panic attacks and fear only compounded the problem. Over the next few months, through this man's wisdom and experience, I learned to reprogram my thoughts so that I would no longer respond to fear. This in turn lessened the reaction in my body. This was such divine intervention, arranged by my loving Heavenly Father. God met me where I was at, and gave me what I needed for further breakthrough in my life.

During this time I found all the Bible verses I could that dealt with fear, and with God's love. I wrote them down on paper and started declaring them over my life everyday. And each day I grew stronger. I experienced freedom from fear and the anxiety attacks, as I firmly stood on the promises and truth of God. I walked through this process day by day, focusing on God's promises, and goodness. I gained emotional strength and clarity. It was a brief reprieve, as Gil and I were about to face yet another challenge.

All the stress we had been living under took its toll on both of us —we were both physically exhausted. Although we were no longer dealing with the intense drama of death or anxiety, our bodies were worn out. I became ill and was physically sick as a result. It seemed every week I was being diagnosed with a new ailment or syndrome. I was in so much pain I couldn't sleep and I was exhausted all the time. So once again, I came face to face with a choice as I lay there. I could choose to walk out what I had learned and now believed about God —that He is my healer and not to give into fear or anxiety. Or, I could buckle, and give in to hopelessness and fear. So I made the choice to declare the promises of God over my body and my life.

Gil was also affected by all of the stress. His health had begun to deteriorate and he began having excruciating hip joint problems. Sometimes the joints were so inflamed that he couldn't walk, and he would have to take time off of work. We didn't know it then, but Gil had a genetic autoimmune disease, and the years of stress triggered the illness. In 1988, Gil went on disability. His doctor advised him to get used to being ill, because it would affect him for the rest of his life. We were told that the illness would get worse as he got older, so it was recommended that we restructure our lives accordingly. It was an intense time and we were frazzled. The last five years felt like one long, continuous battle. Each of the battles we had been though was different, but we began to recognize it was the same enemy beneath them all.

To make matters worse there were people who seemed to come out of the woodwork. They were like Job's friends, thinking they were offering some form of comfort but they only brought judgment and condemnation. We were told things like we were in sin and cursed of God. Or, there must be some root of bitterness, or unforgiveness. We pressed through, and chose to focus on what God was doing and not what people were saying. We stood firm and made the decision to overcome in God's strength. We were thankful for God's hand upon us in this time. His love was apparent as He met us where we were at and continued to bring friends to pray for us and speak blessing and encouragement into our lives.

We now knew for certain that God was our healer and we stood firmly upon that truth. We also learned that a person's body, soul and spirit are interconnected, so we need to take care of all three of these areas. We learned how to maintain healthy bodies through nutrition and adequate rest. We further learned about healing for our souls. Part of that process was learning to deal with the wounds and lies that we had believed, and had even become a part of our identities. It became necessary to admit where we were broken, and let God heal these areas of our souls. Jesus says, "*The thief comes only to steal and kill and destroy. I have come that they may have life, and that they have it more abundantly*" (John 10:10 NKJV).

During this time God taught me how to fight the real of darkness effectively and how to change my mindset so that I would not give into the lies of the enemy. Spiritual strength generated by embracing the truth and promises of God's —word both spoken and written, and then by rejecting the lies and everything else the enemy throws at us.

Gil was now on disability, and very ill. I couldn't work either, so we went deeper and deeper into debt due to reduced income and increasing medical bills. We almost lost our house, which was still in limbo. It was only God's grace that pulled us through and prevented us from having to file for bankruptcy. But then God stepped in and delivered a miracle on our behalf. The lawsuit for our house settled and it was just enough money to pay off all of our debt and get us back on our feet. Through every obstacle and opposition that was thrown our way, we became more firmly established in the goodness and faithfulness of God. The more the enemy tried to destroy us, the more we encountered the amazing awesomeness of God. He backs his Word, and fulfills His promises when we hold on to faith and hope. The truth of these words from Philippians were now firmly rooted into our hearts: *"And my God shall supply all your needs according to His riches in glory by Christ Jesus."* (Philippians 4:19 NKJV)

Chapter Nine

Revival Fire

Yet indeed I also count all things loss for the excellence of the knowledge of Christ Jesus my Lord, for whom I have suffered the loss of all things, and count them as rubbish, that I main gain Christ. Philippians 3:8 NKJV

Therefore, since we are surrounded by so great a cloud of witnesses, let us also lay aside every weight, and sin which clings so closely, and let us run with endurance the race that is set before us, looking to Jesus, the founder and perfecter of our faith, who for the joy that was set before him endured the cross, despising the shame, and is seated at the right hand of the throne of God. Hebrews 11:1-2 ESV

In the early 1990s, we were battle weary but still pursuing God. I was finally starting to feel better —I was still struggling physically, but at long last, there was some stability. I knew I was protected and I knew that God had my back. This gave me confidence to hold on to God's promises and continue to push through the pain and exhaustion I was still experiencing. When Gil and I felt like we could not continue on, God came through for us —He always made a way where there seemed to be no way. We were still in a place where we were fervently seeking God and wanting to understand the spiritual realities of His Kingdom. We knew that if we were to overcome, we needed to familiarize ourselves with the weapons and tools God makes available to every believer. In February of 1991, we decided to attend a conference at the Anaheim Vineyard. It was a cold and rainy week, and I had been sick with bronchitis. I found out later that it had actually progressed to Pneumonia the week we attended the conference. But I was determined to attend the meetings anyway. I would no longer allow another orchestrated obstacle to hold me back. As I pushed myself and persisted, God once again met me in the place of weakness and arranged another divine appointment that changed my life. Even though I was very ill, I pressed through and attended an afternoon workshop by Dr. Jack

Deere. As Jack began speaking, I started receiving revelation in my spirit. I had never experienced the Word of God being brought to life the way I did that day. I felt something inside of me coming alive. Jack had so much knowledge and wisdom but it was infused with compassion, love and hope. As the session ended, I introduced myself to Jack and thanked him. As we chatted, I began to share my heart and then asked some questions about divine healing. As he responded and asked me questions, I ended up telling him some of what Gil and I had been through in the last few years. Before our conversation ended, Jack asked if he could pray for me. In that moment, I felt the love and presence of God come over my whole body, releasing a greater sense of life, wholeness and peace.

The conference was wonderful, and we were awed by what was being released into both the Vineyard movement and into the lives of those who were in attendance. When the conference ended on Friday night, we decided to stay in Anaheim until Sunday. A well-known prophetic minister would be there that evening and we really wanted to hear him speak. Many of the people that came for the conference also stayed for the Sunday services. There was so much faith and expectancy —we certainly didn't want to miss what God was doing! To our amazement, the prophetic minister called us out of the crowd and spoke a word of encouragement to both Gil and I. His words impacted our lives in a powerful way, and imparted so much hope and faith. He began declaring healing over my body and then listed everything that was physically wrong with me. It was amazing because other than Gil and my doctors, no one else knew some of those details. But God knew. The prayer team then took me aside, and then an older gentleman began to pray over me. As he prayed, oil began dripping from his hands —and I mean supernaturally. I had never encountered that before! *What was this*? But as I was being anointed I sensed the presence of God so strongly that my concerns just evaporated. For the next two weeks, I could sense God's Presence in such a profound way that I was trembling off and on all day. I now also had oil dripping from my hands! This was all new for me and

I had never felt God's presence like that before. And then as the conference ended, I realized that the pneumonia and other sicknesses were gone. I was so consumed by God's Presence that I was no longer focusing on how sick I was. I don't really know when it happened, but I was glad that it did! God was teaching me more about His Kingdom and healing. It was all so amazing!

Shortly after the conference, we felt led to make the Anaheim Vineyard our home church. John Wimber became our Senior Pastor, and our understanding of Kingdom of God went to new levels. Even though it was an hour away, we loved our new church and continued growing in the things of the Spirit. During our years at the Anaheim Vineyard, I felt like a lightning rod for prophetic words. Both Gil and I received so much encouragement from many well-known prophetic people. This period of time transformed my life and gave us both a massive infusion of hope. I received words about healing and future ministry. It was such a season of encouragement, and I experienced closeness to God that was more than what I had previously known. I would spend hours and hours crying out to God asking to know Him better. I had so much hunger for the presence of God. Day after day, I was before God, soaking, praying and reading His Word. The obstacles in my life that were designed to snuff the life out of me, just began to disappear as I spent time in God's presence. My mindset changed and I began to have more clarity —I was being delivered and set free! The Word says, *"Submit to God, resist the devil and he will flee from you"* (James 4:7 NKJV). I loved spending time with God, asking Him to reveal His heart to me. As I surrendered more of myself to Him, the realm of darkness had no choice but to retreat.

Gil and I would say (tongue in cheek) that we received our ministry training at "The University of Consuming Fire". Not exactly the seminary we would have chosen all those years ago when we gave our lives over for God's service! But God was forging us by the work of the Holy Spirit. One of the prophetic words that Gil got from a prominent prophetic person was that he was being hammered out on an anvil, and

God was making him into a weapon of choice. Indeed, this is what the last seven years of our lives felt like. Through all the pounding, we were now strong. God took the weak things of the world and revealed His strength.

During our time at the Anaheim Vineyard we identified our gift mixes and discovered how to use them. Gil's pastoral call was confirmed over and over again through prophetic words and personal encounters with God. We grew in our leadership abilities, and received valuable training we would need and use later on.

Day by day I experienced improved energy and health, but Gil slowly got sicker. At one point, it became clear that he was really ill, so after seeing a few doctors, we were told it was some sort of autoimmune disease. At one point he was even told he might have cancer, because he dropped 30 pounds in three months and kept cycling through high fevers. He's always been a thin person, so the weight loss was frightening.

This was such a difficult time for us. We both felt like it was the best of times and the worst of times, intermittent, overlapping and all rolled up together. We experienced so much change and transformation in the middle of more trials and difficulty. We had come out of years and layers of struggles, and now Gil was in need of his own miracle. But this time around, we were ready to do battle and to contend for it. At the "University of Consuming Fire" there are always courses on spiritual warfare. We were in a war for our lives and needed to learn how to do battle. Overcomers always have things to overcome! We had received so many promises and needed to learn how to stand in faith, believe, trust and gain the victory.

"Finally, my brethren, be strong in the Lord and in the power of His might. Put on the whole armor of God, that you may be able to stand against the wiles of the devil. For we do not wrestle against flesh and blood, but against principalities, against powers, against the rulers of the darkness of this age, against spiritual hosts of wickedness in the heavenly places. Therefore take up the whole armor of

God, that you may be able to withstand in the evil day, and
having done all, to stand." (Ephesians 6:10-13)

One of the ways that the realm of darkness distracts
us is through deception and lies. If we buy in to the
lie that there is no way out of our circumstances, the
door to hopelessness is opened. This is why it is
vitally important for us to be rooted and grounded in
the Word of God. We must remember that when the
opposition comes, and when there seems like there is
no way out, God makes a way where there is no way.
His word says, *"No test or temptation that comes your
way is beyond the course of what others have had to face.
All you need to remember is that God will never let you
down; he'll never let you be pushed past your limit; he'll
always be there to help you come through it."*
(1 Corinthians 10:13, The Message)

Gil and I faced many battles together. Each time we
saw the hand of the Lord intervene on our behalf. No
matter what the enemy threw at us, God defended
and protected us every time. Through the entire
process God was shaping us into the people that He

had always intended for us to be. We became living witnesses to the reality that God truly causes all things to work together for the good of those that love Him and are called according to His purposes. Without a doubt, we faced a barrage of circumstances that could have destroyed us. We faced death, we were misunderstood and rejected, and we encountered prolonged seasons of immense difficulty. But the saving grace in all of this was God Himself. He didn't let go of us, and He would not let us give up. He is a really good papa.

There are times when we find ourselves in a weakened state and feel that we can't go on. But what we believe and what we decide during these times is crucial. If we choose to walk through the fire with God, we are on the path to victory. We must decide to stand on His promises and not cave in to despair. Keep fighting the good fight of faith and trust Him —He is fully trustworthy! Believe God for complete victory. Partner with him, and you will find that He is faithful.

I have experienced God's rescue and deliverance over and over again in my life. I love how King David wrote of God's faithfulness in this Psalm:

Our father's faith was in You, over and over they trusted, believing in You and You came through. Every time they cried to You in their despair, You were faithful to deliver them. You didn't disappoint them. (Psalms 22:4,5 TPT)

Chapter Ten

The Death of a Dream

Those who sow in tears shall reap in joy.
He who continually goes forth weeping, bearing seed for
sowing, shall doubtlessly come again with rejoicing,
bringing his sheaves with him.
Psalms 126: 5-6 NKJV

As the years went by, Gil and I experienced the Biblical truth that when you ask Father God for bread He won't give you a stone (Luke 11:11). Every time we found ourselves in desperate need, God came through. Through the years, we also became acutely aware that life can be so unpredictable. There will always be challenges and obstacles and everyone experiences tragedy and loss. It's just the reality of living here on earth. But God is not the author of these circumstances. If I could distill this truth down to one sentence, it would go something like this: The earth is broken, and Father God sent His son Jesus to fix it. This is why God causes all things to work together for the good of those that love Him. There may be times when it doesn't seem like this is true, but as we continue to invite Him into our lives and circumstances, He will act on our behalf. As we stand on His promises and persevere, He will fulfill His Word. Isaiah 55 says, *"For My thoughts are not your thoughts, nor are your ways My ways," declares the Lord"* (Isaiah 55:9 NASB). People often quote this verse as a way to explain tragedy and loss, inferring that God has a greater purpose in mind when people are afflicted with disease and tragedy. But when we read this verse in context, it is speaking about God's mercy, compassion and pardon. It reveals something that is difficult for us humans to wrap our brains around; God is good, and He longs to reveal His goodness to us.

So Gil and I came to believe that God really did have good things in store for us. We were now in a stable place in our lives. We were being renewed and encouraged, as we continued to draw closer to God. We were now serving in our church and excited to be part of an amazing church family. We were also getting lots of valuable training and experience. We were learning so many new things and at one point we began leading a home group.

It was now the spring of 1994, and we had been married for almost ten years. I was in my early thirties and enjoying a season of rest and peace. Around this time, Gil and I began to think more and more about starting a family. Gil and I really wanted to have children. Many of our friends and family were having babies and we wanted our kids to grow up with cousins and friends. Over the years we had also received many prophetic words about our children. When Gil and I prayed about this, we sensed the Lord saying that we would have twins. From the beginning of our marriage however, my doctors advised me against getting pregnant. They said that attempting to have children would not only be extremely dangerous —it would be fatal. So we felt this conflict; we desperately wanted children, but were being told we couldn't have them.

We knew that it was in God's hands, and if it was to happen He would make a way. In May of 1994 I got pregnant. At the moment of conception we both felt the amazing presence of God fill our room. We praised and worshipped God, and declared blessings over our unborn child. We didn't share with anyone what we had experienced. But over the next few days, people began to approach us with prophetic words confirming that I was pregnant —some even said we would have twins. Some began to prophesy over our unborn child, and others had dreams that I was pregnant. These words, combined with our encounter with God only a week earlier, created an even greater sense of confirmation and expectation. We hoped that God was making a way where there appeared to be no way.

From that day forward, I began to sense a change in my body. My heart began skipping and I knew something was different. After two weeks of experiencing these symptoms, I took a pregnancy test and as we suspected, it was positive. Immediately after finding out I was pregnant, I made an appointment with my doctor. Needless to say, he was extremely concerned and explained how dangerous it was for a woman with my heart and lung disease to get pregnant. I told him that I understood his concerns, but said, *"now that I am pregnant I will trust that God will help me through"*. So he referred me to a high-risk pregnancy specialist in Orange County. We wanted to make sure that we were doing everything we could to see this pregnancy through, so we scheduled an appointment with a specialist the following week. After the high-risk doctor examined me, he took Gil and I into his office and said that he had seen many women with various illnesses through their high-risk pregnancies, but he was not aware of anyone with my condition making it through —in this case, pregnancy was considered fatal. He went on to explain that during pregnancy, the lung pressure of the mother normally increases, but since my lung pressure was already high, it would eventually lead to heart and lung failure. He advised us to terminate the pregnancy immediately. Without hesitation, I told him that I believed God would see me through, and we would not abort the baby.

I felt a sense of *déjà vu* in the doctor's office that day —once again fighting for my own life, and now also for my unborn child. But this time around we were stronger and chose to believe God for a miracle. Before we left the office, my new high-risk doctor arranged for more testing and set up more appointments. But before I saw the doctor again, I became very ill. I could hardly breathe and my heart was continuously skipping. I had bad morning sickness as well. I couldn't eat, and once again, it was difficult for me to get out of bed.

More weeks had now passed and I continued to feel worse every day, even hour by hour. It was time to see the doctor again, so Gil and one of our friends helped me down the stairs and into the car. I had been using oxygen continuously for the past couple of weeks, and took a portable tank with me for the hour-long drive to Orange County. Once I got to the doctor's office, we were rushed back to the ultrasound room. Within a few minutes, the technician found a heartbeat. As she pointed it out on the monitor, we were awestruck. What an amazing moment! But as she continued the ultrasound, she suddenly gasped and then exclaimed, "Oh, there's another heartbeat". So we discovered that I was carrying twins. We were able to see them and hear both their heartbeats on that visit. My heart was overjoyed! People had given us prophetic words about twins. Seeing the blips on the monitor and hearing their heartbeats made us want to fight even harder for their lives.

As we returned home, my physical condition was deteriorating. So we made phone calls to friends and other in our church family, asking them to pray and stand with us. We wrote letters to some of the internationally known prophetic people that had spoken into our lives over the last few years. Within days, people in our church initiated a corporate fast, contending for our unborn children. Our home group and some of the pastors from our church continued to fast and pray for us. Over the next few days, I was not doing well at all. I felt like I was dying again, and my doctor agreed.

Gil and I set a specific date; we had to make a decision one-way or the other. Many people were fasting and praying on that day. At about 12 noon, the high-risk specialist called Gil saying that the ultrasound revealed some abnormalities —there was only one amniotic sac, and even with identical twins there should be two. He went on to say that even with healthy women he advises to terminate the pregnancy because a miscarriage is inevitable, and in my case a miscarriage would prove fatal. He also said that the lung pressure in my heart had increased dramatically, and this was putting a lot of strain on my already weakened heart. He advised us to terminate the pregnancy at once. The final thing he said to Gil was "You will have to make the decision. Lisa is not willing to make it. If you don't, you will not only lose the twins, but you will lose Lisa as well." I also began to feel intense heart pain on that day. My lips were now blue all the time, and I had trouble breathing. So

Gil made the most difficult decision of his life. Although none of this made any sense to either of us, we made the decision to move forward to save my life. I didn't understand why this was happening —it was absolutely devastating.

Early the next morning we drove to the hospital. I was completely awake through the whole procedure because I was not able to have general anesthesia (due to the heart and lung disease). There were a number of people in the operating room as they began the emergency procedure: A cardiologist, the high-risk pregnancy specialist, an anesthesiologist and a few others I did not know. They were watching my vitals closely because my blood pressure was down and my heart rate was really slow. But I felt God was with me through the whole procedure. I could feel His presence in the room. When it was all over they wheeled me to my room to rest and recover. Within the hour I felt energy return to my body and I was relieved to feel alive again. My doctor kept me overnight, and then I was released in the morning. At this point, I felt so much better physically that I didn't feel an emotional loss or disappointment. But the next few weeks were extremely difficult. I began to mourn the loss of our twins and cried constantly as I went through the grieving process. It was unlike anything I had experienced before.

Through the process of mourning, the Lord gave me names for our boys. They were not names we would have picked out but I believe they were the names God chose. The first was Anthony. As I looked up the meaning of the names I discovered that Anthony means *"highly praiseworthy"*. The second name was Joshua, which means, *"The Lord saves"*. As I went through this process the Lord said to me, "Praise me because I'm worthy to be praised and I will be your salvation." This encounter with God released peace and began the process of healing.

There were a few events in this process of healing that were pivotal. At one point I received a letter from one of the prominent prophetic ministers that had been praying for us. He told us that God was saying, "Grace, grace, grace" to both Gil and I. He also said that what the enemy meant for evil, God would turn around for His glory." We embraced God's grace and continued on our journey of healing. I remembered the words of Corrie Ten Boom: "When a train goes through a tunnel and it gets dark, you don't throw away the ticket and jump off. You sit still and trust the engineer."

Gil dealt with the termination of the pregnancy differently than I did. When he came home from the hospital he was extremely angry. He went into his office and told God he was done being a Christian. He yelled at God and informed Him that he no longer wanted to be in ministry. He asked God to just leave him alone. So God left him alone for a few days. But on the third day, as Gil was sitting at his desk, he suddenly felt someone come up from behind and wrap their arms around him. The presence and love of God was so powerful that it melted Gil's heart. He wept for hours, and asked God to forgive him. This encounter was unusual for Gil because up until that time, God mostly spoke to him through scripture, words or pictures. But God met Gil right where he was. He went down into the pit Gil was in and touched the deep wound in his heart. Gil had a tangible experience with God that transcended the physical realm. As Gil poured out his heart to Papa God that day, the Lord asked Gil to trust Him. So Gil chose to trust, even though he was still in emotional anguish, and though the disappointment still remained, he was now ready to walk through the process of healing. This ultimately paved the way for Gil to press into the call and purposes God had for him up ahead. It was a difficult time for both of us, but we chose to rest in God's love and mercy. We took our time and did what was necessary to heal.

Three years later, on Mother's day 1997, Gil and I were at church. We were both on the prayer team, and as I began praying for a young mother as the service ended, something completely amazing happened. As I finished praying for this young lady, I suddenly had a vision of two little boys that completely caught me off guard. It was so vivid; one came running toward me saying, "mommy, mommy." He was so cute with little brown corduroy overalls on. The other one had on a t-shirt with little blue-jean shorts. He shyly peaked out from behind a tree and slowly came over and wrapped his arms around my leg. As the vision ended, I was stunned. It was so unexpected, but I was so grateful to God for his amazing Mother's Day gift to me. He showed me that my children were happy and living a wonderful life with Him. I experienced such deep healing love from my heavenly Father on that day.

We had come to accept that we would not have children (at least not with us here on Earth). We still did not understand why things happened the way they did, but we came to accept that we may never understand on this side of heaven. But I still chose to believe that God is good. Just as the prophetic minister declared, God took what the enemy intended for evil, and was now turning it around for His glory. I continued to stand on God's promise; *"All things work together for good to those who love God, to those who are called according to His purpose"* (Romans 8:28).

Since that Mother's Day in 1997, I had another vision of my sons in heaven and saw what they were doing. They were about 17 years old and one was painting beautiful landscapes and sunsets. The other was building and fixing things. This made me smile because Gil is very artistic and a painter, and I love to build and fix things. When God communicates with me in this way, it happens in an instant. It's what we now call "downloads". It's amazing and so different from the usual process of human imagination. If we discount the various ways that God can speak to us, we will miss out on so much!

Chapter Eleven

Total Brokenness

...to comfort all who mourn, and provide for those who grieve in Zion – to bestow upon them a crown of beauty, instead of ashes, the oil of joy, instead of mourning, and a garment of praise, instead of a spirit of despair. They will be called oaks of righteousness, a planting of the Lord for the display of his splendor. Isaiah 61:2-3

The year we lost our twins was extremely difficult. We each dealt with the loss in different ways. My grief revolved around the death of a dream. I wanted to have a family that laughed together, played together, cried together, prayed together and ministered together. I wanted to have children of my own and nurture them in God's love. But I would never know the joy of having children who were passionate about serving God and helping others.

That dream was now dead along with the hope of what I thought my life would look like. I was heartbroken. Gil on the other hand was becoming more and more angry. The loss of our sons was bad enough, but he was now plagued by the fact that he was forced to make the decision to terminate the pregnancy. A pervasive sense of guilt grew to the point that it enveloped him.

There were so many questions we needed answers to; *did we not fight hard enough or pray hard enough? Did we miss God? What could we have done differently?* We also went through a time of disillusionment with personal prophecy and prophetic words. In the years and months before I was pregnant, we had received so many clear and unsolicited words about children and even twins. There were so many supernatural events that no human could have orchestrated. *Was it all wrong?* We both went through a time of confusion and uncertainty in regard to hearing God. *Had we really heard from Him or were we deluded?*

Losing the twins placed a huge strain upon our marriage. Because we both dealt with the pain and loss differently, it magnified some of the issues already present in our marriage. Our personalities were so different, as well as our likes and dislikes. We seemed to be opposites, but instead of recognizing this as a positive, the enemy capitalized on it and we grew distant. During this time Gil was still so angry about what had happened, and even though he couldn't admit it at the time, he was still angry with God and with me. He began to pull away emotionally and I felt more and more alone as the gulf between us continued to grow. Although I tried, I just didn't know how to repair the rift. During this time, Gil was away at seminary for a few days during the week so we did not see each other often. But seminary actually made things worse as he was introduced to various schools of thought regarding the Bible and Jesus. Many of the things that Gil believed were called into question, and he felt his foundation of faith slowly eroding. As a result we drifted further and further apart. We were both processing a devastating loss in different ways, and it became difficult for either of us to see beyond our own pain. Gil became increasingly frustrated and disillusioned without recognizing what was happening. Although he experienced that encounter with God (as He embraced him after terminating the pregnancy), gut-wrenching grief and disillusionment took hold of his soul. Gil was now in a crisis of faith that would take time to recover from.

As the hopelessness increased we made a decision to separate. We both had things in our lives that needed changing. I began crying out to God asking Him to save our marriage. I was totally broken and felt as though I had lost everything. I would never have children (at least here on earth), my marriage seemed to be over, and hope for ministry was gone. I no longer felt like I had a purpose, and worst of all I could no longer sense the presence of God. *What was my life about? What were the last 10 years about?* It seemed that God went to great lengths to save my life but now I wondered how I ended up like this. Something, somewhere must have gone wrong, but what? I didn't understand. Everything was gone —taken away. This was my dark night of the soul.

Grief consumed us, blinding us to the grace and goodness that was all around us. We knew we had to make a decision —we had to choose; would we stand on the faithfulness of God that had gotten us through every other storm in the past? Or would we yield to grief and open the door to a lifetime of hopelessness?

Gil and I decided to go with God. But we needed to be able to trust Him again. We recognized that if there was a problem, or if there was blame to assign, it would be with us, not God. So with that as our starting place, we began to slowly dig ourselves out of the pit we were in. We kept reminding ourselves that He was still God and He is good. This became the foundation on which we rebuilt our relationship with each other, and with God. It was the truth we kept coming back to, and despite the anger, grief and uncertainty, it became the anchor that steadied us through this fierce storm.

"I would have lost heart, unless I had believed that I would see the goodness of the Lord in the land of the living" (Psalm 27:13 NKJV).

Over the next few months, the Lord showed himself to be fully deserving of our trust. With each step forward, faith and hope were gradually restored, but not just to the levels we had in the past. Our faith and hope were now somehow stronger. It had been tried in the fire, and as we chose to trust, we experienced more and more restoration in our souls.

In the mid 1990's there was an outpouring of the Holy Spirit known as "The Toronto Blessing." It became a worldwide move of God and many believers were positively impacted by it. It was also instrumental in putting our marriage back together. Gil was still at seminary and meetings were being held every night at Mott Auditorium in Pasadena. I would sometimes drive out and meet Gil at these meetings that were filled with the presence of God. Night after night, our hearts were slowly tenderized, to the point that we experienced freedom from the sorrow and pain we had been carrying. The more time we spent in God's presence, the more freedom we experienced. The love of God was evident in such a tangible way and I was touched in ways that I still can't describe to this day.

The love of God heals broken souls! Jesus said that He was sent to proclaim freedom for prisoners (Luke 4:18). This aspect of Jesus' ministry has never stopped and it is still available to anyone who wants it today. Gil and I found ourselves in a season where the prison bars were being demolished, and we were being set free. Forgiveness began to flow into our marriage like a flood, filling the chasm that separated us. The Holy Spirit also identified patterns in our lives that needed to be changed. Gil and I recognized that our differences were intended to complement each other, so instead of trying to change each other, we began to appreciate our differences.

Joy was now a part of our lives again. I have never laughed so much in my life! Laughter dissolved away the grief and sadness that had become a part of our identities. God is the giver of every good and perfect gift, and the gift of laughter transformed our hearts. We began to hear God's voice again and received more words about our destiny and what God had planned for us up ahead. Our hearts were opened once again, and ready to trust.

After all that we had been through, there were still times when we felt like we were disqualified from being used by God. But God, rich in mercy and full of love, continued to reveal His heart and plans for us. He had prepared us for ministry. It's true; *God uses the foolish things of the world to confound the wise* (1 Corinthians 1:27). So we were fully qualified! Time and time again He reminded us that He had a good future planned for us. During these pivotal months of personal renewal, we realized that we needed the continual infilling of God's grace flowing through our lives in order to be effective in life and ministry. One definition of *grace* is "*God's empowering presence*". A lifestyle of connection and communion allows God's empowering presence to flow through our lives. Perhaps more than anything else, we had learned how vitally important it was for us to guard that connection.

Chapter Twelve

For Such a Time as This

*For if you remain silent at this time, relief and deliverance
for the Jews will arise from another place but you and your
father's family will perish. And who knows but that you
have come to royal position for such a time as this?*
Esther 4:14

Gil and I still felt like we were the most unlikely
people to be used by God. Although we had both
overcome so many obstacles and grown immensely,
we would have never identified ourselves as senior
leaders. Gil was somewhat introverted by nature, and
speaking in front of groups was not within his
comfort zone. But God had a plan and we gradually
began to understand why he called us into ministry.
The very things that we once perceived as deficiencies
had now become areas of strength. God's strength

was revealed through our frailty. God is a redeemer, and Jesus came to redeem us —not only in regard to our eternal destination, but also in regard to our lives in the here and now. He takes the broken areas of our lives where the realm of darkness has tried to cut us off at the knees, and He flips it. Again, I will refer to my favorite verse, Romans 8:28 *"All things work together for good to those who love God, to those who are called according to His purpose."* There's a key for us here, hidden in plain sight. It's for those who *love* God. This is the trump card for the believer. Nothing is wasted! So God turns tragedy into triumph for those who love Him.

So Gil and I began to embrace the call of God on our lives with a confidence that we did not have before. A section of a book by Bill Johnson, *"Hosting the Presence"*, explores the call of God on the nation of Israel. Bill says, "God chose Israel. They were the least of all, the most insignificant of all, the weakest of all nations. There was nothing in their natural qualities that made them stand out from any other people group. But there was one thing that set them apart. It was the presence of God". In Exodus 33:14 we see it boldly declared, "My presence will go with you, and I will give you rest." The glory of God and His manifest presence would be the distinguishing mark that set them apart".

As I look back to 1983, I see that God marked us on that day in Gil's parent's living room. We gave Him permission to do whatever was necessary to make us the most useful for His kingdom. As we surrendered our lives, He took us up on our offer —God never declines an invitation! There were many years of training, refining and persevering, but we finally sensed the hand of God nudging us forward. We were transitioning now into a different phase of life. Over the next decade, Gil and I served at a few churches in our community. Our level of involvement varied at each church, but we always had a heart for people to come to know God in a deep and personal way. As we took on various leadership responsibilities, we gained valuable experience that would be needed down the road.

2004 began an even better phase in our lives. We began attending a large church in town, and once again served in ministry. But this time, as more opportunities came up, one thing led to another and we were both asked to serve on staff. It was an amazing opportunity —we found ourselves coming alive and feeling like we were finally doing what we were created to do. At one point, I was asked to share my testimony at the Sunday services. Before this, I had not done much public speaking and I was reluctant to share my story with so many people. I discussed this with God saying, *"I'm not sure I want to share my story"*. Immediately I heard Him say, *"It's not just your story, it's My story."* Once again God gently nudged me and I stepped into what He had prepared for me. God moved powerfully on that Sunday, and I was absolutely amazed at how my story affected others. In the days that followed, I reflected on the lives of some of the heroes of the Old Testament. People like Joseph who went from the prison to the palace, and Moses who went from the palace to the wilderness for his training. One of my favorites is Esther, an orphan girl descended from captives, who rose to the rank of Queen of Persia and saved her people from mass annihilation. Although their journeys were very different, God used each of these people for His purposes. We all have different paths, but all of us have a common purpose —to love God and to bring Him glory. *"For we are His workmanship, created in Christ Jesus for good works, which God prepared beforehand that we should walk in them"* (Ephesians 4:10). As we journey through life, walking closely with God, our individual destiny and purpose unfold. What an amazing privilege, as we walk hand in hand with our awesome God!

In the spring of 2008, the Lord directed us to take a break from church ministry. We had been serving at our church for over four years, and were enjoying it immensely. This new direction was surprising, but we both sensed a strong leading from God. So as we handed off our responsibilities and stepped down, we took some time to rest, and sought the Lord for direction. We were in a new season and were anticipating His leading. One Saturday morning, at the beginning of summer, as Gil woke up and opened his eyes, the name of a book popped into his mind. It was a book that he had never heard of before. He was shocked, and not used to hearing so clearly. Gil found the book on the Internet, printed it, and then began reading. Because we no longer had any church responsibilities, he had the luxury of taking the rest of the day to read and relax. The book was written in 1906, at a time when God was powerfully impacting the American church. I also had a similar thing happen earlier in the week; I was at a Christian bookstore and felt impressed to buy a certain book, by an author I would not normally read. That Saturday morning, I went upstairs where Gil was already reading and I read a few sentences from the book to him. Gil looked at me with a shocked look on his face. At that very moment, he was highlighting the very same thing in a book written over 100 years earlier. The sentences were not verbatim, but they were identical in concept, referring to the people of Israel and the presence of God. Just then, the presence of the Lord filled the room, and we went down on our knees and began to pray and worship. Throughout the rest of that morning and afternoon, the Lord continued to speak to us, giving us a blueprint for what he wanted to do through us, for our city and the surrounding area. This day marked the beginning of a much-welcomed season of visitation.

During this time we were leading a small mentoring group. We were meeting with four couples that were hungry for God and wanted to grow in their relationship with Him. On that Saturday as Gil and I worshiped and prayed, the Lord told us that this mentoring group would form the core of a new church plant. At first we were hesitant because we had never thought about church planting. Not to mention, we had been a part of enough church plants to know that it was hard work. We also felt like we didn't really have what it takes to be senior leaders. But as the days went by, God kept confirming. At one point it was so clear, that all that was left for us to do was to say "yes" or "no". We knew that if we said "no", we would be forever haunted by the *what if* question. The turning point came a few weeks later. As we discussed it, I asked Gil what we had to lose if we said "yes". He said "well, if we fail, I guess all we lose is our pride —and we can always get that back". We both laughed, and then made the decision to say "yes" to God.

We were excited and apprehensive all at the same time. Once again, we came face to face with our own limitations and weakness. But we remembered how God had come through in the past, whenever we surrendered our weaknesses to Him. Pastor Bill Johnson says, "When you're willing to do what you are unqualified to do, that's what qualifies you." So just like Moses, we asked, "Lord, let your presence go with us. We do not want to go unless your presence is with us." And so we responded to God's leading. That week, we received a number of prophetic words from ministers who did not know us, or what was happening in our lives. In one instance the minister said, "You have tried to start your ministry in the past —it wasn't a false start, it just wasn't the right time. Now is the time." Gil and I were also having dreams and various other confirmations that continued for weeks. We were convinced that God was in this, and that He was truly leading.

Before we had our first meeting as a brand new church plant, we continued to meet with our little home group on a weekly basis. We spoke to the group about what was happening to us. We weren't sure what they would say, but they all responded positively. In the weeks that followed a few more people joined the group. It was such an exciting time!

We were now in a season of visitation. God's presence and leading were so tangible. The Holy Spirit was speaking to both of us so clearly. The pattern that began that Saturday morning continued for Gil. Over the next few weeks, on each successive Saturday just as he woke up, the Holy Spirit would speak to Gil. He didn't know it at the time, but these downloads formed the core values for our soon-to-be church plant. These values are as follows: The first thing was, *"Focus on My presence, not on programs"*. Secondly, *"Advance my Kingdom and I'll build your church"*. Third was *"Measure success by how you invest in people, not by numbers."* Fourth, *"Keep a light touch on people. I will bring them to you. You will help heal, empower and equip them, and then I will take them and put them where I need them."* Last of all, the Holy Spirit asked Gil, *"Will you let me be in control?"* Gil took a couple of days to answer. He knew what God was asking, and he wanted to be able to follow through if he said yes. A few days later he did say yes. Gil and I, along with our core group didn't want to do church as usual. God was showing us that He was changing the face of the Church, as we know it. He was creating a new wineskin to contain and release what He wanted to do in our area. It was more than just about doing church, it was about *being* the church. We weren't sure what all of this meant at the time, but we knew just enough to keep saying yes! We were excited and knew God would continue to bring definition to the blueprints as we continued to say yes to Him. God gave us a deeper understanding of His Kingdom during that time, which has become the foundation of all that we do.

Our mentoring group grew and we became a non-profit church on Aug 18, 2008. We had our first official meeting toward the end of September of that same year. In the meantime, Gil and I began to read

"When Heaven Invades Earth" by Bill Johnson. We weren't familiar with his church or ministry at the time, but as we read through this powerful book, we recognized the same concepts that God was revealing to us. We were excited to find that there were other believers out there who had already grabbed hold of these truths. At the time, we didn't know of any group that was so like-minded. As we finished reading the book, we felt drawn to the Bethel movement, so we decided to attend the Open Heavens conference in October of 2008.

At our first visit to Bethel Church in Redding, California, we were greatly encouraged and had a divine appointment that connected us with the Global Legacy Network. Global Legacy is a relational network that connects, encourages, and equips revival leaders throughout the world. It was at this first conference in Redding that we found our tribe and connection. Gil and I have been back up to Redding at least a dozen times since, and every time we come back encouraged and strengthened, with a clearer understanding of what God is asking us to do.

In these last few years, God has continued to bless us with favor and grace. His love has been unfailing; He brought us through every obstacle and challenge, and has enriched our lives to the point that we are different people than when we first got married. We now have a wonderful church family that passionately pursues God. As a result, people are encountering His love and goodness. Lives are being changed as hearts are transformed.

Through this long journey, we learned that life has its ups and downs, but no matter what life throws at you or how dark and how hopeless things may seem, God will always be there with you! *He promises to never leave you or forsake you* (Hebrews 13:5). And even through the trials and troubles we can find hope. Even through those things that test our faith, we find that testing produces patience and the patience produces perseverance. James 1:2-4 states, *we must be willing to let patience have its perfect work, that we may be perfect and complete, lacking nothing.* This was such powerful revelation that has guided our lives, and produced fruit for the Kingdom.

Life can be compared to a race, but it's more like of a long-distance event as opposed to a sprint. So we need to pace ourselves, position ourselves to persevere, and then not give up.

"Therefore we also, since we are surrounded by so great a cloud of witnesses, let us lay aside every weight, and the sin which so easily ensnares us, and let us run with endurance the race that is set before us, looking unto Jesus, the author and finisher of our faith, who for the joy that was set before Him endured the cross, despising the shame, and has sat down at the right hand of the throne of God."
(Hebrews 12:1-2)

God has a plan and a destiny for each of our lives. We need to be patient with the process and continue to pursue Him. When we pursue relationship with God we discover how much He loves and cares for us. We realize that He truly knows and understands us, and has a plan for each of us. It is through this journey of discovery, that true peace and rest is found.

I began this book by asking questions. As a young woman I was so fearful when faced with the reality of death. If we don't ask questions, we probably won't get answers. So I encourage you to ask your own questions: *What is the plan he has for your life? What is your destiny? Can you trust Him even if it doesn't look the way you think it should look? Especially if it doesn't happen within the time frame you expect it to?*

Jeremiah 29:11 reveals a powerful promise: *"For I know the plans I have for you, declares the Lord. "Plans to prosper you and to not harm you, plans to give you hope and a future."*

This is a passionate revelation of God's love and intentions toward each of us. God truly causes all things to work together for good for His children. When we choose to walk in trust and faith of that truth, we are on our way to apprehending all that He has for us.

As for us, Gil was healed of the autoimmune disease that plagued him for decades. He is now stronger than ever and doing great. I also have an active, full life now. My faith in God has given me the strength to persevere through extremely difficult circumstances, and now I am enjoying the fruit of that labor. Gil and I stand as reminders to the truth that you also can have that same level of breakthrough. Just begin to position yourself before God and ask him for it. Jesus says, *"Ask and it will be given to you; seek and you will find; knock and the door will be opened to you. For everyone who asks receives; the one who seeks finds; and to the one who knocks, the door will be opened."* He goes on to say, *"Which of you, if your son asks for bread, will give him a stone? Or if he asks for a fish, will give him a snake? If you, then, though you are evil, know how to give good gifts to your children, how much more will your Father in heaven give good gifts to those who ask him!"* (Matthew 7:7-11).

I hope that as you have read my story (and God's story!) that it has awakened spiritual hunger in you. I pray that you will seek God with all your heart, soul and mind. And I pray that you will never give up as you seek Him and His purposes for your life. He will meet you in every circumstance —I am one of millions of witnesses from the beginning of time that testify this is true. It is my desire that as you passionately pursue Him, you will encounter His goodness all the days of your life!

Here is what I learned through it all: Don't give up, don't be impatient; Be intwined with the Lord. Be brave courageous, and never lose hope. Yes, keep waiting — for He will never disappoint you!

(Psalm 27:14 TPT)

Prayer For Salvation

If you want to know the same God who delivered me from death and put a new song in my heart, and if you want to experience the love of God and His presence in your life, than please pray this prayer with me:

Father God, please reveal Yourself to me in a personal way. Let me know your loving presence. I surrender my life to you. Thank you Lord Jesus for dying on the cross for me. Please forgive me for all my sins. I now give my life fully over to you.

Holy Spirit be my comforter and counselor and fill me each day with your presence.

If you have prayed this prayer and would like more information on how to start your new life following Jesus, please visit our website: www.revivehope.net

About Lisa A. Bujanda

Lisa and her husband Gil are the Founders and Senior Leaders at The Call of Temecula Valley Church. Lisa's passion is to impart hope to anyone who needs it. And no matter how difficult circumstances may be, to encourage others to persevere and not give up, to press on, run the race, and finish well! She also loves to pray for the sick and see them healed, delivered and set free.

Her favorite verse is Romans 8:28 "And we know that in all things work together for good for those who love Him, and are called according to His purpose. "

Lisa also has a ministry called Revive Hope. Revive Hope is dedicated to bringing healing through hope and encouragement.

Visit our website at: www.revivehope.net

Made in the USA
Charleston, SC
15 December 2013